# *famous* WAYS TO GROW OLD

*a collection of letters*

compiled and introduced by
PHILIP BRISTOW

*Foreword by HRH The Duchess of Kent*

© 1989 Philip Bristow

**Published by Age Concern England**  
Bernard Sunley House  
60 Pitcairn Road  
Mitcham, Surrey CR4 3LL

ISBN 0-86242-087-3

Editor  David Moncrieff  
Design  Eugenie Dodd  
Copy preparation  Vinnette Marshall  
Production  Joyce O'Shaughnessy  
Cover photography  Sunil Gupta  
Cover props supplied by Allders of Croydon  
Picture research  June Guiness  
Printed by Grosvenor Press  
(Portsmouth) Limited.

♦ — *Photo Credits* — ♦

Cover: Camera Press, London – *Barbara Cartland (Norman Parkinson); The Rt Hon Edward Heath; Mother Teresa (Karsh of Ottawa).* Topham Picture Library – *The Rt Hon James Callaghan; Stewart Granger; Dame Vera Lynn.*  
Age Concern England – *Page 101;* BBC Copyright – *Pages 121, 127;* Camera Press – *Pages 6, 45, 65, 83, 89, 107, 115;* Popperfoto – *Pages 53, 57, 69, 73, 97, 109;* Ben Rice – *Page 49;* James Sharkey Associates – *Page 29;* Syndication International – *Page 103;* Topham Picture Library – *Pages 31, 35, 37, 41, 43, 47, 51, 55, 61, 63, 67, 71, 77, 79, 81, 85, 87, 91, 95, 111, 117, 119, 123, 125, 129, 131;* WRVS – *Page 113.*

# Contents

*To Emma and Bill, for patience in adversity.*
*With one bound . . . . .*

York House
St. James's Palace
London S.W.1

    I am consistently delighted and full of admiration at the extent of the work undertaken by the Age Concern movement to improve the quality of life for both today's older people and those of tomorrow. As Patron, I am particularly pleased to have the opportunity to write the Foreword to <u>Famous Ways to Grow Old</u> and to support its positive message that there is so much satisfaction to be found in the years following retirement.

    The letters contained in the collection make entertaining and inspiring reading, demonstrating that old age is no obstacle to enjoyment and fulfilment. They act as a timely reminder of the real contribution older people can make to society in terms of their skills, time, energy and wisdom.

    Over a period of almost 20 years, I have been proud to see Age Concern develop into the largest, single independent provider of direct services to older people in this country. It has been my privilege on many occasions to meet many members of our community whom the charity exists to serve. As the organisation celebrates its Golden Jubilee I would like to extend my best wishes for the next half century of caring and I hope that this book will stimulate and encourage all its readers.

<u>PATRON</u>

# Contributors

**70**
Hallowes, Odette

**112**
Hearst, William Randolf

**109**
Heath, Edward

**114**
Henderson, Roy

**94**
Hepple, Norman

**95**
Heston, Charlton

**101**
Hobman, David

**58**
Hodge, Sir Julian

**53**
Home of the Hirsel, Lord

**65**
Hume, Cardinal Basil

**120**
Hunter-Tod, Air Marshal Sir John

**79**
Kerr, Deborah

**115**
Jakobovits, Lord

**34**
Leverhulme, Lord

**61**
Longford, Elizabeth

**72**
Lutyens, Mary

**84**
Lympany, Moura

**47**
Lynch, Jack

**117**
Lynn, Dame Vera

**128**
Madden, Admiral Sir Charles

**104**
Manwaring, Randle

**122**
Mitchison, Naomi

**119**
Murdoch, Richard

**66**
Murton of Lindisfarne, Lord

**42**
Norman, Vice-Admiral Sir Geoffrey

**57**
Powell, Enoch

**36**
Powell, Professor Hugh

**103**
Proops, Marjorie

**54**
Pyke, Magnus

**63**
Rose, Sir Alec

**71**
Scarman, Lord

**131**
Seyler, Athene

**85**
Shultz, George P

**30**
Sirs, Bill

**76**
Slattery, Rear Admiral Sir Matthew

**125**
Smith, Ian

**102**
Solti, Sir Georg

**45**
Soper, Lord

**130**
Stack, Prunella

**90**
Stokes, Lord

**51**
Sutherland, Dame Joan

**83**
Teresa, Mother

**52**
Thorneycroft, Lord

**99**
Tonypandy, Viscount

**78**
Toye, Wendy

**129**
Weinberger, Caspar W

**38**
Welensky, Sir Roy

**55**
Whitfield, June

**127**
Wing, Anna

# ♦—*About the Author*—♦

Philip Bristow served in the Royal Navy and subsequently owned several small boats, as well as a thirty-five foot seagoing yacht.

After founding the annual reference book, *Bristow's Book of Yachts*, he was attracted to the inland waterways of Europe. He has travelled extensively on these and has produced a number of guides for the canals, rivers and coasts of the continent.

Philip Bristow is married and lives in Hampshire.

# introduction

We stood on the bridge at St Jean-de-Losne and watched our 81-year-old friends move out of the lock into the Canal de Bourgogne. They looked back to us and we waved goodbye as they set off on the long cruise home. On returning to our own boat we found an English couple standing enviously alongside, attracted by our flag. He volunteered the information that he would have loved to cruise the inland waterways of France, but felt it was too late to consider it now. We enquired whether he had been ill, but this was apparently not the case at all; it was merely that he and his wife were both over 60 years of age....

These opposing attitudes to the retirement years set me wondering why older people should have such different approaches to the onset of old age. Why is it not more widely understood that ageing occurs in relation to one's attitude to it? It seemed to me, as I turned the matter over in my mind that summer's day, that as much guidance was needed at the sunset of life as at the sunrise. Who might provide such guidance, who might help and advise?

This thought gave me the idea of writing to famous and distinguished men and women over the age of 60 for advice and guidance on a suitable approach to growing old. I must admit that I was somewhat doubtful whether such eminent people would reply. I took names at random. From a tentative start of writing about a dozen letters at a time, I was immensely gratified at the response and kindness shown. The warmth of interest in helping others to enjoy their retirement years was most impressive. I wrote over 250 letters to prominent men and women all over the world, among them African leaders, South American sportsmen and Scottish peers. I received replies to about half; a very satisfying response rate since such distinguished people must receive many requests of all sorts and have many demands made upon their time.

A few of those I approached wrote to say that they were much too busy to contribute to my book, clearly indicating their own approaches to the onset of old age. However, since they were obviously still so active I thought how kind it was of them to reply at all. A very small percentage of the people I wrote to sent gruff rejections, as though they were not happy themselves in retirement.

Fame does not provide a shield against unhappiness, illness or old age after all; although it could well provide opportunities for enhancing retirement activity.

It might be thought that many of the contributors to this book are privileged people with far more opportunities open to them for coping with retirement and possessed of advantages not available to the 'average' older person. Whether or not this is true, many of them certainly did not start out in life with any better prospects than the rest of us, and their respective claims to fame are due to personal achievement.

Because of their wider knowledge and experience, I believe that the advice so kindly given is enlightening and helpful, not least the warnings of the undesirability of doing nothing in retirement, and being too concerned with one's own problems.

# ♦— *Introduction* —♦

My standard letter to potential contributors asked for words of advice and guidance to help those seemingly unable to cope with growing old. I told them that I was compiling a book of opinions that was intended to help prevent older people from drifting into boredom and despair and influence them to try and remain bright, optimistic, cheerful and active like so many of their contemporaries.

The replies I received make up this book. Some are reproduced in full, others are edited a little; all the letter-writers have kindly consented to the publication of their contributions. It is fascinating to read so many different views on how to seek and, perhaps, discover the gift of contented retirement years and I hope that readers will find the material helpful and inspiring.

Many of the opinions expressed in the collection of letters which follows assure us that retirement should be, and can be, the happiest time of our lives. Opinions vary, of course, as one would expect. For some, it is a generally unhappy state – a traumatic experience; others express the belief that the greatest of gifts is life and that those blessed with a full quota of years should enjoy every day under the sun. They suggest we should be grateful for our long lives and look upon every year as a bonus. Happiness can certainly be achieved in retirement and if you are not happy it is never too late to do something about it – as the letters show.

## ♦— *I*ntroduction —♦

When asked on his 80th birthday, 'How do you feel being 80 years old?', Winston Churchill is reported to have answered 'Considering the alternative, very well'. STEWART GRANGER puts it more succinctly when he writes 'Getting old is a bitch but it's better than being dead'.

It is undoubtedly possible to achieve active contentment in retirement and many of the letters included in this collection show the way. Our minds are generally capable of continuing to function through the advancing years and it is widely believed that mental activity promotes and preserves physical health. DAME FRANCES CLODE'S advice is 'Keep a sense of humour, and laugh whenever you can. Banish the word frustrated, if your spirits are low, do something; if you are doing something, do something different'.

Many of the letters stressed that in order to enjoy old age you must do something, anything. For instance, FIELD MARSHAL LORD CARVER'S advice is to 'keep busy and interested in something other than yourself and your own problems'. We are advised to keep the mind fully stretched; to learn something new everyday.

People who are in occupations where they have simply carried on working regardless of their 60th or 65th birthday can be viewed as living proof that activity is an excellent antidote to the passing years. Such people rarely bother to take heed of the onset of ageing because life's signposts don't signal a change of direc-

14

tion for them at the traditional retirement age, as is the case for most of us. Age has made very little difference to their way of life. For instance, LORD DELFONT, who happens to be 79 years of age, writes: 'Much as I would like to help with your book I do not consider that I am old – not yet! Just approaching middle age'.

Continuing involvement and interest is likely to keep you young in spirit. The lately retired President of the United States, for instance, has a characteristic belief that, whatever your age, you can always be young at heart. The White House confirmed this when it wrote: 'Rather than have a 77th birthday, President Reagan celebrated the 38th anniversary of his 39th birthday'.

President Reagan did not, of course, retire at 65; indeed, he was not elected President until he was 69. If your job continues regardless you are generally able to go on yourself as well, as many of the letters reveal. But it is not only such people who have the opportunity of utilising their later years so fully. Many people have retired to become hooked on a new interest that has far exceeded the interest they ever displayed in their working lives. There is little reason why anyone should not find such a hobby.

In regular employment our mental apparatus is being fed a daily input and responses are active. Following retirement this input is reduced and some alternative stimulant is needed to take its place or sluggishness and apathy develop. 'Men last longer, in better health, if they continue active', says PROFESSOR HERBERT C BROWN, who celebrated his retirement by winning a Nobel Prize award. BARBARA CARTLAND is convinced that 'the older one gets, to feel young and remain young, one must keep working'.

From other letters it is clear that many of the contributors believe that the more you can involve yourself in some rewarding retirement occupation, the less you will be concerned about your age and the less preoccupied you are with that subject the better will be your chances of finding a rewarding activity with which to fill your time.

It has to be accepted that the majority of retired people do find it difficult to ignore old age, but to have reached retirement age doesn't necessarily mean that you are old. You don't know what it is like to be old until you are old. As LORD SOPER observes, 'I knew very little about it until it happened to me'.

It seems that few people realise, until they retire, that a considerable number of the interests that occupied their day were associated with their work and that, at a stroke, these concerns vanish on retirement. In such circumstances, they feel alone on a stage from which all the other actors have fled. They seem to have stepped out of the busy environment in which they knew their value and influence into the 'world of retirement' which seems to offer nothing but emptiness and rejection.

For those who feel like this SIR BERNARD BRAINE hits the nail on the head when he remarks: 'The enemy, of course, is loneliness and the feeling that one is no longer needed. It need not be so. We can, if we choose, reach out to other people. After all there are plenty of good causes and voluntary organisations in our midst crying out for helping hands. The old, better than the young, should know that giving is more rewarding that receiving'. MONICA DICKENS' counsel is to turn yourself outward to the lives of other people and make yourself pleasant to be with.

'Most helpful of all, read', says REGINALD BEVINS when discussing his way of tackling loneliness, and there are a number of similar recommendations. Sir Bernard Braine writes 'with a good book one is never alone', whilst from LORD HOME comes the advice to have 'three books handy on which to ring the changes'.

Libraries and bookshops are fascinating places and it is a pity not to take full advantage of them. If your mind goes blank when standing in front of the bookshelves it is a good idea to keep a notebook of recommended reading handy. Apart from the Bible, about the only advice on suitable reading contained in the collection comes from DOUGLAS DILLON who says 'Tennyson's great poem *Ulysses* can provide a constant source of inspiration to the elderly'.

It is essential that action is taken before feelings of loneliness become entrenched. ROY HENDERSON advises people to prepare for old age 'well before you become pensionable', whilst PROFESSOR CYRUS GORDON remarks that 'it is an error to dream of a distant retirement paradise'.

Pre-retirement associations are opening in growing numbers and pre-retirement education is being increasingly promoted today but interest in such instruction seems not to be high.

Subjects covered in such courses often include health, finance, personal relationships in the home and community, living accommodation when retired, interest and leisure occupations. As GEORGE SHULTZ says, 'if you're willing to learn, there are new things all around you. The act of learning keeps you young and vital'. In any locality you can see 70 year olds who are bumblers and 80 year olds who are bright, cheerful and active.

Dr Peter Hanson's book, *The Joy of Stress*, states that the sudden silence gained by retiring from a demanding job into a life of idleness usually causes death or senility within two years. This opinion is supported by SIR KENNETH CORK when he says 'I think if I were to stay at home all day and do nothing but plod around the garden I would be dead within three months'.

A number of the contributors sound a warning to those who retire proclaiming their pleasure at the prospect of freedom and do not perceive the associated dangers of drifting into boredom, deteriorating relationships and despair. SIR JULIAN HODGE, for instance, whose initial ambition was to make himself financially secure for a leisured retirement, soon realised that he needed to go on working in order to enjoy his sunset years and was therefore quick to observe that those foolish enough to give up all their activities are sowing the seeds of disaster. A bank manager friend of his suddenly relinquished an active and exciting life to watch television. He barely lasted 12 months. A senior police officer friend retired, never to do another stroke of work. 'I don't think he lived two years. I could go on citing people who suddenly turned off any strenuous mental activity to the complete detriment of their physical well-being'.

# ◆— *I*ntroduction —◆

The very act of exploring the various options open on retirement is stimulating and refreshing. The letter-writers recommend a variety of activities and there are, of course, many charities which would be grateful for help. All charity shops need people to serve, to price goods and to do the books. Thousands of volunteers are required for all sorts of permanent fundraising activities in addition to the annual street collections and house-to-house appeals. Many organisations need drivers to help run such projects as meals-on-wheels and books-on-wheels.

CASPAR WEINBERGER supports such activities, recommending 'try to be as helpful as possible to others . . . because it tends to take a lot of one's time and attention and therefore keep one's mind off . . . day-to-day worries'.

Just as some organisations provide opportunities for work, others offer the chance to learn. As EDWARD HEATH remarks, 'institutions like the Open University have a wide range of courses geared to the more advanced in years'. Alternatively, home hobbies recommended include needlepoint, tapestry, embroidery, picking the losers in the daily papers (although this might turn out to be a rather expensive hobby!), jam, marmalade and jelly making and keeping family scrapbooks.

Many retired people who never had the time or opportunity to travel find great satisfaction and contentment in doing so, particularly since special concessions are available to those who can travel out of peak season.

# ♦— *Introduction* —♦

Moving is a momentous event at any age but different considerations arise following retirement. Many retired people discover that their house and garden have become too big, entailing too much work. Consequently, many people are tempted to move to a smaller house and some, perhaps foolishly, move right away to what they consider to be a more congenial environment. However, by no means everybody considers that such a move is a good idea. The letters include a number of opinions on the subject.

'Do not leave the place where you have lived while working, and where all your friends and acquaintances are, to move to a remote district or the seaside where you know no one and where most of those living there are even older than you', is the advice of ADMIRAL SIR CHARLES MADDEN. Another significant comment on the subject comes from SIR ROSS CHESTERMAN, who writes: 'In growing old, I myself made many bad, avoidable mistakes. My first wife and I retired from a satisfying and busy academic life in London to what appeared to be a dream cottage in beautiful country, yet found ourselves cut off from all our friends and interests'. Apart from the value of the close proximity of old friends, the very fabric of life is made up of trivial but important daily contacts, with the butcher, the garage man, the newspaper boy, the man across the road and so on – a hundred familiar faces of all ages.

So, think before you move! Don't be persuaded that gardening is a chore that you should give up. Health can be improved with the interest of a garden. Surrender a large garden by all means but perhaps only in exchange for something smaller. RICHARD

MURDOCH says 'maintaining a small garden is good for one's health and peace of mind'.

Many of the letter-writers pay tribute to family and friends. SIR MATT BUSBY comments 'my family and my grandchildren help to keep my spirits high'.

It may be that it is still the minority of husbands who help with domestic chores but those who do so generally find a happier acceptance by going along with established routine; many derive interest and enjoyment by learning to cook. Stewart Granger writes 'I love to cook and entertain my friends – to give them something they can't get at any restaurant: home cooking'. More words of wisdom from AIR MARSHAL SIR JOHN HUNTER-TOD are: 'Don't inflict oneself on one's spouse, eg go one's own way for lunch; get it and have it when you feel like it – who said I married him for better or worse, not for lunch? Take over a part of the chores; eg do all the washing up or learn to cook'. In a similar vein, the advice from Reginald Bevins is: 'Go walking for an hour, thereby sweetening relations between yourself and the wife...; do a bit of shopping'.

Not everyone is so understanding and many people seem to expect life to go on as before. Readers are advised to stop thinking of their imaginary problems or their past glories and stir themselves to do something. 'The old can easily become very boring if they only talk about the past' says RANDLE MANWARING. The advice from Dame Frances Clode is: 'Try not to trot out too many reminiscences or to repeat your best stories'.

Your local church is likely to be the centre of much helpful activity, quite apart from providing that special something that belief in God brings many of us. A good many of your problems could be answered there, worthwhile tasks might be found together with new interests and new friendships. Peace is there for the seeking. Sir Ross Chesterman advises 'build up new relationships – perhaps by joining a church'.

Many of the contributors pay tribute to the value of their religious beliefs and the influence of the church in their lives. LORD MURTON, for instance, says 'Those whose beliefs are strongly rooted in Christian doctrine are best able to cope with the onset of old age'.

Eubie Blake (the composer of *I'm just wild about Harry*) is reported to have said, when he was 100 years old, 'If I had known I was going to live this long I would have taken greater care of myself'. If he was implying that he had not bothered much about his health it sounds as though Eubie Blake must have come from good stock.

Heredity is often an important ingredient in determining how long and happily we live, and a number of the letters pay tribute to long- living parents. However, whether you have such tenacious forebears or not, and generally assuming that you are not under medical care, you can probably feel better by asking more of yourself, both physically and mentally. Many medical authorities and a number of the letter-writers offer the opinion that better health, at any age, could be ours if we persuade ourselves to make an effort to seek it, rather than accepting that we are as we are and that there is nothing we can do about it. A healthy old age is within the reach of most of us.

With the right motivation it would seem that age is no bar when it comes to persuading ourselves to do a little more. LORD JAKOBOVITS writes of Golda Meir who, when she was summoned to be Israel's fourth prime minister at the age of 71, was a sick and tired woman, but was instantly rejuvenated by the adrenalin of the enormous new responsibilities thrust upon her. We cannot all be prime ministers, but a strong desire to achieve something constructive can be a spur to better health.

Quite a number of the letters mention the important part that health plays and the need to preserve it as far as we are able. LORD CALLAGHAN says: 'The most important foundation for an enjoyable old age is good health. Blessed with that, all doors remain open'. BILL SIRS offers the following advice: 'Age is relative to condition and we can all do more to ensure that our bodies are in good condition. That in turn allows us to take part in leisure activities that make retirement a joy'.

The more you walk and exercise the better your health is likely to be. If you have got out of the habit of walking it would be wise to make a start as soon as you can. At first you may be a bit slow but regular daily exercise soon brings improvement. If you can stroll along amidst grass and flowers and trees, where you can feel close to God, it will benefit you mentally and physically.

Advice to move about more vigorously may not be easy to accept but it is worth trying to swing one's arms and put one's shoulder back just a little bit more. One of the most noticeable things about people who have retained their sparkle and remain fully active and alert to an advanced age is that they always seem to be on the move.

Belief in the value of exercise needs to be strongly held if tempting alternatives are to be resisted. 'The greatest temptations in modern living are the cosy armchair and the television set' says Lord Murton. Indeed, television watching comes in for a fair amount of criticism from some of the contributors. 'Sitting in a lounge chair before a TV is no way to grow old' says PRESIDENT GERALD FORD.

Exercise is very likely to make us feel better. Another equally important – but less strenuous – way of feeling good is to take pride in our appearance. As SIR HUGH CASSON advises, 'keep clean and as elegant as you can afford in your appearance and your setting... and you may get more visitors, it sounds flippant, but isn't'.

Attention to diet is also recommended; eating and drinking should only be done in moderation if maximum health is to be enjoyed. Lord Home suggests that every glass of wine drunk should be matched by one of water.

# ♦— *I*ntroduction —♦

Good health and a sense of physical well-being are likely to enlarge your life and consequently improve your perception of the possibilities open to you; and how we think can affect how we feel. 'You should have good feelings about things and people,' writes LORD FORTE. 'If you do, you have a chance of being healthier. If you do not, debilitating tension arises'. This theme is developed by Lord Callaghan, who directs our attention towards the younger members of society. 'Listen to what the young have to say' he advises. If you have skills and experience that would benefit younger people, share them. To keep in touch with the younger generation is a means of keeping yourself young. ANNA WING recommends: 'Don't cut yourself off from young children, they recharge the batteries if you see them for short sessions'.

Advice to seek out younger companions, to indulge in more vigorous exercise and other recommended activities is all very well provided your state of health allows you to take advantage of such advice. But whether we are fit or whether we are ailing, TERENCE CUNEO asks, 'is it inevitable that we must lie back in gloomy resignation and let so-called old age take over?'. He goes on to say, 'we've all got to fight this . . . . and we can'. 'We all of us have uncharted and untapped strengths', says Anna Wing.

If you have been ill for twenty years, have had three heart attacks and a triple by-pass operation and have faulty eyesight and difficulty in walking, you would undoubtedly consider that you had cause to be thoroughly fed up with life. Yet 81-year-old CARL ALBERT, ex-Speaker of the American House of Representatives, whose letter reveals this personal catalogue of misfortune, goes on to say: 'In spite of all this... dissatisfaction with living has never entered my mind. I like to read, I like to study, I like to live. While I suppose I have reached old age I never worry about it'. Best-selling author, CATHERINE COOKSON, who is 81 and has been dogged with serious ill health for years, writes that she spends most of her time 'in bed . . . or in hospital, but as long as my mind is active I'll carry on; and there'll be another two books next year'.

If battles can be won by ignoring the enemy then Carl Albert and Catherine Cookson are victorious in their attitudes. They prove that fighting old age and a preoccupation with growing old need not necessarily be a conscious battle by any means so long as your mind is actively engaged and certainly away from your own problems.

'No-one can expect an ageing body to function like that of a young person's but the mind can and should continue to work and the best way to make it work is to keep it working' is MARJORIE PROOPS' comment.

A signpost to making it work is provided by SIR ROY WELENSKY when he writes that 'the elderly . . . . want and need compassion and friendship'. Despite the obvious desirability of trying to meet this need, it is hard to really believe that just providing compassion and friendship and offering to help somebody worse off than yourself will be enough to get your mind working. Surely, you may think, in order to solve your own retirement problem of boredom you need something more than this – more of a proper job in fact. But the answer to this doubt has been provided by many people who were equally sceptical at first, but who found that because the *giving* of compassion and friendship benefits the giver as much as the receiver, it really does provide personal fulfilment, the opportunity to fight, and to keep the mind working. Perhaps this collection of letters may influence you to help yourself by helping others and to realise that the thousands of causes crying out for your help and support are there for your salvation as well.

As MOTHER TERESA writes, 'Growing old is a gift from God'. Surely we are intended to enjoy that gift.

*Philip Whistan*

## Stewart Granger.
## Born London, 6 May 1913.

Stage and film actor.
Film credits include:
*King Solomon's Mines,*
*The Prisoner of Zenda*
and *Bhowani Junction.*

Dear Mr Bristow

Physically I'm getting really old, (76 last birthday);
spiritually, emotionally I'm 45. I can't believe I'm that
ageing old poop that looks back at me out of the mirror.
I'm not rich, (I lost most of my money in '74 ...., reaction
to the bloody Arabs putting up the price of oil 400 per
cent, blast them to hell).

Yes, I think that is what keeps me young, vehemence,
anger – outrage at injustice; and playing tennis with a
pro who doesn't hit the ball too far away from me (or he
doesn't get paid!).

I'm a cook. I love to cook and entertain my friends – to
give them something they can't get at any restaurant:
home cooking. Study cooking - it comes naturally to me –
but if not, study it. Learn something, try writing. I wrote
my biography when I was 67 – didn't think I could write
but I did it and it wasn't bad. (Sparks Fly Upwards – try
and get a copy – bad language I'm afraid.)

Relationships: make friends, try for a few especial
friends, so that you can experience new things together.
So sometimes you are bored? (Thank God for TV.) That's
life – stop being sorry for yourself. Getting old is a bitch
but it's better than being dead.

Best wishes,

Stewart Granger.

## Bill Sirs JP. Born 6 January 1920

General Secretary, Iron and Steel
Trades Confederation, 1975-85.

Dear Mr Bristow

My approach to life has always been to care for my physical well-being. It is so important to all human beings to be able to retire and grow old and continue to be active, thereby slowing down the ageing process both in looks and physical capability.

Age is relative to condition, and we can all do more to ensure that our bodies are in good condition. That in turn allows us to take part in the leisure activities that make retirement a joy.

A healthy approach to life also eases mental strain that affects some older people who cannot face the change from an active working life.

One cannot outline all the activities available to older people but as the intention should be to live as long as possible, with trouble-free health, it is essential that we maintain our interests or create some to keep mind and body healthy.

A final point I would make is that people should be prepared for retirement and growing old, and whilst there are many of us who are capable of preparing ourselves, there are vast numbers who need help to do so.

Yours sincerely

*Bill Sirs*

## Barbara Cartland D St J.
## Born 9 July 1901.

Best selling authoress of
over 450 titles;
500 million copies
sold world-wide.

◆ ◇ ◆

*Dear Mr Bristow*

*I shall be eighty-eight on the 9th of July this year and many people ask me how I am managing to do so much work — ten books already this year — and as you know I am the best-selling author in the world; I will tell you my secret.*

*The answer is quite simply because I believe in my vitamins and take a great number of them.*

*I am also quite convinced that the older one gets, to feel young and remain young, one must keep working. I do not mean a nine to five job. What I mean is what they call in America 'Go, go, go!' all day!*

*We have the terrible habit in this country of pushing people, soon after they are fifty, into Old People's Homes, giving them nothing to do, and*

31

sitting them down in front of the television until they die.

This means they are not using their brains, and the brain gradually atrophies. Then they become really senile long before they should do so.

My Mother, who kept going all the time, lived until she was ninety-eight, and drove her car until she was ninety-five.

I am working harder today than I have ever worked in the whole of my life, simply because I am using my brain.

What you want is plenty to do.

There are a thousand Charities longing for you to help them, if you do not need to earn money. Any Political Party will receive you with open arms.

As I have said so often before, go to your Town Hall, and let them give you a list of all the different organisations. Join the lot!

When you have found a few friends whom you really like, you can drop the rest.

But you yourself, will be keeping young, keeping energetic, and keeping charming.

There is nothing more boring than old people muttering into their knitting or just staring into space.

What you need every day to keep young, is first of all Vitamin E, which prevents you from having a heart-attack.

Also Selenium prevents you from having cancer. Nutrimental, which as I have said, carries oxygen to your brain and makes you feel as if you are on Concord, and to these add two Cardio-2-Forte.

If you take all these and use anti-wrinkle cream on your face you will feel and look young for ever.

Yours sincerely

*[signature]*

*Dear Mr Bristow*

*My advice to those who seem unable to cope with growing old, is to keep themselves fully occupied. If, on retirement, they sit back and do nothing, they will find this is the quickest passport to the grave.*

*There is an enormous amount of voluntary work available to the old and there should be no excuse for sitting back and doing nothing.*

*Yours sincerely*

*Leverhulme.*

## John Arlott OBE.
## Born 25 February 1914.
Former cricketing journalist
and broadcaster.

Dear Mr Bristow

Once when George Bernard Shaw was asked to name the consolations of old age he remained silent until his questioner repeated the question. Then he said 'I am still trying to answer that question'.

There is no escaping old age, but it is a fortunate man who can find work such as writing, drawing or painting that he can do at home. The mistake is to think that doing nothing is its own salvation.

Yours sincerely

John Arlott

## Professor Hugh Powell MA, DLitt.
## Born 4 September 1912.
### Emeritus Professor of German, Indiana University.

Dear Mr Bristow

On the whole, intellectuals, especially academic people, appear not to have to cope with boredom when they retire. Indeed, in many cases release from responsibilities of regular employment gives freedom to pursue their interests more consistently.

It is the nine-to-five employee, whether 'manual' or 'professional' who on retirement is apt to have difficulty in adjusting and combating the feeling of no longer being of use or wanted, and who finds it hard to deal with the 'vacuum'. The individual has to accept that aging is inevitable; that it happens to everybody who survives the fifty mark. For those who sorely miss the companionship of colleagues it is especially important that they examine their needs and plan to meet these. It could mean joining clubs, playing bridge, whist, darts, bowling, skittles and so on. I have frequently seen older people show undisguised joy on meeting their friends. The energy no longer directed to a regular job ought to be used in other ways. Here, it seems to me, *routine* is especially important too. Household chores, regular meals, errands, the daily walk or other forms of exercise, visits to the local library to thumb through newspapers and magazines or borrow books can help fill a day purposefully. The time passes more quickly when organized, and time unnoticed spells serenity. Knowing when you awake in the morning that there *are* things to do, some less congenial than others, it is true, and that if you don't do them, things may not be so nice for others – this gives you a sense of belonging and of usefulness.

So much depends on the environment. An understanding and affectionate family or neighbour can make a significant difference.

Yours sincerely

Hugh Powell

**Rt Rev Lord Coggan** PC, MA, DD.
**Born 9 October 1909.**

Archbishop of York, 1961-74;
Archbishop of Canterbury, 1974-80.

Dear Mr Bristow

My advice, put very briefly, would be:

'Look up to God, for strength and peace,
Look out for someone in need whom you
can help'.

That way we do not drift or deteriorate.
We develop and mature, (like good
wine).

All best wishes.

*Donald Coggan.*

# Sir Roy Welensky PC, KCMG.
# Born Salisbury, Southern Rhodesia,
# 20 January 1907.

Heavyweight Boxing Champion of
Rhodesia, 1926-28;
Prime Minister of Rhodesia, 1956-63.
Now lives in England.

Dear Mr Bristow

As I am rising 82 and of moderate means (I receive no pension as an ex-Prime Minister), I felt perhaps that I could make a contribution on the subject of old age.

First of all, let me make it clear that I am badly crippled with arthritis, and the prospects of a wheelchair loom closer and closer, and like most people of my age, I have suffered a host of illnesses that have left their mark. But the thing which stirred me sufficiently to give tongue on this subject were the figures quoted by Mrs Edwina Currie about the number of old people in this country. She said in an article that I read in The Daily Telegraph 'people are living longer – we will shortly have 4.5 million over the age of 75 – a million over 85, and half a million over 90 years old'. I mention these figures, merely in support of the fact that as a nation we are getting older, with all that that entails for the elderly.

Perhaps I should make it clear that my own experience in this country has left me with the impression that the vast majority of younger people are only too anxious and willing to help the older ones – this ranges from physical assistance in the streets to help in the homes. I have had some experience of travelling in the world, but I firmly believe that this country does as much for the elderly as any country that I have visited.

Now to get to the other side of the coin. What is it that elderly people want, and what do they need? I make no apology for saying that the vast majority of the elderly want and need compassion and friendship, but perhaps most of all they need help to overcome their handicaps, physical and otherwise. Let me give an example or two of the things that strike me as being so obvious that something should be done about. The first is the question of entry to buildings. If I need medical or dental treatment, the first query that my wife makes is, is the office or surgery on the ground floor. If the answer is a staircase, it's out as far as I am concerned. Recently I had to visit a physician at a recently constructed hospital, and an excellent place it is, but to my surprise I discovered that in the waiting room there was not a single chair that I could sit in and get out of unaided. Surely this kind of thing is obvious, and should and could be rectified easily. I could go on giving examples, but I think I have made the point.

The other aspect which concerns me is the high price of the various aids to one's mobility that are advertised. In my own case, in addition to having to instal a type of lift, I had to find the means to purchase an electric chair (not American style), but a chair which assisted in getting one to stand up. The cost of this item was in excess of one thousand pounds. One does not have to be a Solomon to recognise that most elderly people suffer a reduction in their income, when they are no longer able to earn money. In my own particular case, I am fortunate. I have two daughters, who do help my wife in the task of looking after me. Personally, I have the greatest, sympathy for all elderly people who are living alone, and have to fend for themselves all the way. I am indeed grateful to Mrs Currie for drawing the attention of the people of this country to the growing problems of old age. Four and a half million people over the age of 75 in the near future is a sobering thought.

Yours sincerely

Roy Welensky

**Douglas Dillon. Born Geneva, 21 August 1909.**

United States Ambassador to France, 1953-57;
United States Under Secretary of State, 1958-61;
United States Secretary of the Treasury, 1961-65;
Chairman, United States and Foreign Securities
Corporation, 1967-84.

Dear Mr Bristow

Healthy survivors, I believe, have an obligation to their friends and loved ones who have gone before to live out their lives with joy and gratitude for all of life's many blessings.

Tennyson's great poem 'Ulysses' can provide a constant source of inspiration to the elderly, and I recommend it to all who begin to feel the burdens of age.

With best wishes,

Sincerely,

*Douglas Dillon*

## Douglas Fairbanks Jr KBE, DSC.
## Born New York,
## 9 December 1909.

Actor; writer; producer;
company director.
Film credits include:
*Little Caesar* and
*The Prisoner of Zenda.*

Dear Mr Bristow

Health is luck and healthy parents. My mother lived to
her eighties but my father died when he was 56; he
smoked incessantly and had hardening of the arteries. I
trained and kept fit when doing swashbuckling films
and have been interested in skiing, water skiing, tennis
and swimming and it is necessary to take exercise.
Eating in moderation is beneficial. I pass on the advice
my father gave me, everything in moderation, nothing
in extreme – let your own discretion be your tutor.

Those who have far more money than they need should
consider giving to those in need.

Sincerely

41

# Vice Admiral Sir Geoffrey Norman
### KCVO, CB, CBE.
## Born 25 May 1896.

Chief of Staff to C-in-C Mediterranean, 1948-50.
Secretary,
National Playing Fields Association, 1953-63.

Dear Mr Bristow

As an old man who spent nearly 40 years in the Silent (so called) Service I'm not likely to make a very intelligent reply to your letter. But here goes.

Health, once lost, is a tragedy – so keep fit. Elderly men tend to over-eat – their wives, or widows more especially, tend to eat too little. Walking is good for everyone – not racing along but fast enough to make one feel one's muscles. This applies particularly after an illness or accident.

Keep in touch with the younger generation. Not necessarily one's own family but neighbours' children. My wife's and my own age adds up to 179 years. Our garden rang with childish voices – all from local but unknown families – at our Annual Easter Egg Hunt – the only trouble was to provide enough 'eggs' to go round and to hide them before the young eyes spotted them.

Gardening is now our chief hobby. While I can, I supply the bulk of the labour.

So my advice is to keep up one's hobbies – and indulge in some reading there hasn't been time for to date.

Yours sincerely

Geoffrey Norman

— ◆ ◇ ◆ —

**Dame Peggy Ashcroft DBE.
Born 22 December 1907.**

Film and stage actress;
Director, Royal Shakespeare Company.
Film credits include: *The Nun's
Story* and *A Passage to India.*

— ◆ ◇ ◆ —

*Dear Mr Bristow*

*How difficult to write any advice or guidance on the
question of growing old. It seems to me an inevitable
ill that we all have to face, and I find very little to
be said for it.*

*Of course those of us who are lucky enough to
have grandchildren or young relatives can find much
satisfaction in their interests, and my advice to those
who are not lucky in that respect is to take as much
interest as possible in the various matters that concern
the young, so that Age Concern could become
Youth Concern.*

*But finally everyone suffers from the growing
dependence on other people. Anything that one can
do to reverse that and give help I am sure is of
enormous importance.*

*Yours sincerely*

*Peggy Ashcroft*

**Carl Albert. Born Oklahoma, 10 May 1908.**

Speaker of the United States House
of Representatives, 1971-77.

Dear Mr Bristow

Now past eighty years of age I have ....been dogged with illness for more than 20 years. I had a heart attack at age fifty-eight and have had two since that time. I had a triple bypass three years ago. I have had faulty eyesight and a certain loss of hearing for some time. Walking has become difficult.

In spite of all this, fear of dying or dissatisfaction with living has never entered my mind. I like to read, I like to study, I like to live. While I suppose I have reached old age I never worry about it.

Sincerely

Carl Albert

## The Revd Lord Soper MA, PhD.
## Born 31 January 1903.

Methodist Minister;
President of the
Methodist Conference, 1953.

— ♦ ◇ ♦ —

Dear Mr Bristow

It is always important, especially for minsters of the Gospel,
that what they say should come out of their experience.
Observing this rule would probably curtail many a sermon, but
in the matter of getting old I do know what I am talking about
because I am an old man.

I suppose the first thing that needs to be said is that the process
of ageing is strictly personal. I knew very little about it until it
happened to me. Maybe I can be of some help to other old
people if I write down one or two of the lessons I have learned
and, indeed, one or two of the encouragements I have found.

First and above all there are two great enemies of old age – one
is boredom and the other is inactivity. It is of the greatest
importance that when 'working days' are over something
constructive must be put in their place. That cannot easily be
done if left to the time of retirement. It needs to be prepared
for. I have found in the continuation of preaching and the
continued involvement in the church a safeguard against
boredom. Of course, preaching is not everyone's vocation, but
there are many church activities in which you could take a part

and a constructive one at that. Have you thought about that possibility?

I have not found it so easy to deal with the increasing inactivity which is geared to physical deterioration, in my case arthritis. So let me tell you, if I can, how I have tried, however imperfectly, to face it.

It helps to know that you are not alone in this condition, and quite truthfully I have found faith in a future which goes far beyond my ending of this life on this planet. It helps to persuade me that this physical life here may be a house which is crumbling but 'in my Father's house are many mansions' and, by His grace, it will be my happiness to live in one of them.

Just a postscript. It is easy to feel unduly sorry for yourself. My wife and I are blessed with many grandchildren. Being glad for them is a marvellous tonic.

Yours sincerely

*Donald Soper*

— ♦ ◇ ♦ —

## Jack Lynch.
## Born 15 August 1917.

TD (Republic of Ireland)
1948-81;
Taoiseach,
1966-73, 1977-79.

— ♦ ◇ ♦ —

Dear Mr Bristow

One's approach to growing old is very subjective and depends largely on one's own background.

I had a varied life – starting as a civil servant, then a practising barrister, then an active politician and on retirement from politics in 1981, at age 63, as a non-executive director of a number of business companies. Each phase presented its own challenge. In the years ahead full retirement will present a new challenge.

In meeting it I can draw from the experiences of a varied career and do things that I did not have time for before. For example, I can swim more often in my club pool. I can walk more in the Dublin mountains, 15 minutes' drive from my home, selecting my own time, and I can travel abroad for pleasure more often. The number of fundraising activities in which I am involved has increased.

My visits to the theatre, opera and ballet are more frequent and I can play, more often, records from a fairly good selection, including modern and folk. There is nothing like music to revive memories. My garden enjoys a little more – not very expert – attention and I read a wider selection of books. Occasionally I record a book for the blind – there is a cassette library for the blind in my native city of Cork.

Growing old can be as fulfilling and rewarding a phase in one's life as any other. It is up to oneself.

Yours sincerely

Jack Lynch

## Gwen Ffrangcon-Davies.
## Born 25th January 1891.

Actress. Principal successes include:
Tess in *Tess of the D'Urbervilles*, Elizabeth Barrett
in *The Barretts of Wimpole Street*
and Anne of Bohemia in *Richard of Bordeaux*.

*Dear Mr Bristow*

*I have no magic formula for overcoming the belief of age — except 'don't accept it'. I was brought up never to celebrate birthdays — we just didn't have them in my family.... 'another year gone' is not a helpful thought.*

*So, 'don't accept it' is the best advice I can give.*

*Sincerely yours*

Gwen Ffrangcon-Davies

## Sir Reay Geddes KBE.
## Born 7 May 1912.

President, Abbeyfield Society;
Chairman,
Charities Aid Foundation.

— ◆ ◇ ◆ —

Dear Mr Bristow

To the growing majority of elderly people doctors now give the chance of a 'Third Age', after childhood and a working life, and before the possible 'Fourth Age' of dependence.

As the 'Third Age' can offer some 30 years of interest and reasonable activity it would seem worth mastering.

The limitations of ageing are not diseases; it is how each of us feels that matters. So it is good to ask ourselves the question; what can we look forward to?

Some of us do change but most of us seem to become more like ourselves, perhaps kinder and more interested in others. However, some are tempted to become boring, procrastinating, irritable, self-centred: these need to take care, before the habit becomes established, or they will in time blame others for the loneliness that they themselves create.

Most of us bring into retirement a number of skills, interests, hobbies, friendships and acquaintances, with time to develop them. While some enjoy the growth of a spiritual or contemplative life, more need recreation, experiment and often find an unexpected aptitude – a friend recently gave a

49

first exhibition of his paintings on his 80th birthday: many of them were sold.

Many find satisfaction in applying long known skills and experience to help and encourage others who are starting in life.

The more we help our older friends to sustain a life of some interest and activity, the more others will be there to help us when the time comes. Communities need ever more voluntary effort and those who provide it, within their own competence, can find that very rewarding.

These random thoughts are not just drawn from the experience and inexperience of one man in his late 70s – that would be presumptuous. They arise from the privilege of watching the success of residents and volunteers in the Abbeyfield Societies' houses spread around the country; there are more than 1,000 of them. They are created, sometimes with the help of Government or Local Government, by voluntary effort, legacies and so on. Once established they are kept up to scratch and running costs are met by the residents themselves, perhaps with the help of social security allowances. One recent incident may tell their story and show their spirit. The 1988 fund raising ITV Telethon attracted the attention of Abbeyfielders, who not only raised £100,000 for other causes, but knitted some 8,000 warm woollen blankets for the needy overseas.

Yours sincerely

## Dame Joan Sutherland AC, DBE.
## Born 7 November 1926.

Soprano.
International Opera Singer.

*Dear Mr Bristow*

*In short, my advice would be to remain interested in finding out more about the world we live in and its people. Also, one has to develop and extend the hobbies one may have had through life — in my own case gardening, needlepoint and, of course, music and reading. After all, old age comes to all of us and we have to cope. Just pray to God that we are well enough to enjoy our leisure years!*

*Sincerely*

51

## Lord Thorneycroft CH, PC Born 26 July 1909.

Member of Parliament, 1938-1966.
President of the Board of Trade, 1951-57;
Chancellor of the Exchequer, 1957-58.
Secretary of State for Defence 1964;
Chairman of the Conservative Party, 1975-81.

Dear Mr Bristow

There can be a joy in old age – but to find it is as much a matter of luck as of application. I was lucky. I had always tried to paint and old age brought me the chance to do it.

There comes a point in everyone's life when the scene begins to fade. We come down from whatever was the mountain that we climbed; we descend into the valley. The tumult and the shouting dies. We are no longer even thought of as indispensible. Life slows to a gentle stroll and even at that pace we tire more quickly.

For me I could just devote more time to handling a pencil or playing with paint and water upon paper. You don't need to be a great artist to enjoy yourself. You can sit and gaze at the beauty of the world and try to sketch it. But supposing you either can't or don't want to learn to paint. The important thing is to do something. Above all, it is important to learn about something. Happily in this country there is a vast range of adult education. The best place to go is to the Public Library. The Enquiry Desk will furnish you with a list of almost endless opportunities from a study of church glass to fly fishing. An older person will surely find something to occupy his time and incidentally to meet others engaged upon the same pursuit. With a little bit of luck some joy can be found for almost everyone as they grow older. It is not a disaster but an opportunity.

Yours sincerely

## Lord Home of the Hirsel PC, DL.
### Born 2 July 1903.

Member of Parliament
1931-45, 1950-51, 1963-74.
Leader of the House of Lords and
Lord President of the Council, 1959-60;
Secretary of State for
Foreign Affairs, 1960-63;
Prime Minister
and First Lord of
the Treasury, 1963-64.

Dear Mr Bristow

I think that the difficulty in answering your question will be that my answers would be inapplicable to the majority of people, eg birds, butterflies, flowers and fishing. They are my therapies — or even, always having three books handy on which to ring the changes, or to drink a glass of water for every one of wine!

Yours sincerely

Alec Home.

Dear Mr Bristow

As long as one cheerfully accepts Shakespeare's dictum that 'all the world's a stage/and all the men and women merely players', there is no reason why a sensible person should not enjoy at least five of his seven ages with zest and gusto. (I have not much to say of muling and puking at one extreme or pretending that being 'sans eyes, sans taste, sans everything' is much fun. But since I am over 80 you would not expect me to, would you?)

My advice to my fellow men and women who are growing old too – and who isn't? – is not to expect too much of one's well worn body as we set sail through 'second childishness'. After all, we were not all that clever during the first.

Yours sincerely

*Magnus Pyke*

**June Whitfield** OBE.
**Born 1 November 1925.**

Actress: stage, screen
and television.

*Dear Mr Bristow*

*The only advice I can really give is to do all you can to keep healthy and busy. Don't spend too much time — if any — thinking about getting old. You are as young as you feel!*

*Best wishes,*

*Yours sincerely*

*June Whitfield*

# Field Marshal Lord Carver
### GCB, CBE, DSO and Bar, MC.
## Born 24 April 1915.

Soldier.
Chief of the General Staff, 1971-73;
Chief of Defence Staff, 1973-76.

*Dear Mr Bristow*

*Thank you for your letter. I don't think I have any more to say on the subject than, 'Keep busy and interested in something other than yourself and your own problems'.*

*Yours sincerely*

*Michael Carver*

## Enoch Powell PC, MBE, MA.
## Born 16 June 1912.

Professor of Greek,
University of Sydney,
NSW, 1937-39.
Member of Parliament, 1950-87.
Minister of Health, 1960-63.

— ♦ ◇ ♦ —

*Dear Mr Bristow*

*I am myself a lucky man in that in old age I remain inquisitive and interested in a number of absorbing subjects. I doubt, however, whether, by describing this, I can assist others to discover qualities which they do not possess.*

*Yours sincerely*

◇◆ ◇◆ ◇◆ ◇◆ ◇◆ ◇◆ ◇◆ ◇◆ ◇◆

# Sir Julian Hodge FRSA. Born 15 October 1904.

## Founder and Chairman,
## Commmercial Bank of Wales.

◇◆ ◇◆ ◇◆ ◇◆ ◇◆ ◇◆ ◇◆ ◇◆ ◇◆

Dear Mr Bristow

When I was young I decided to retire at 50, as I felt sure that by the time I reached that age I would be able to do so. But the older I got the more interested I became in my work, and the harder I worked the better I felt. In fact, it would be true to say that the only time I felt under the weather was when I went on holidays.

This made me realise that an active mind helps to keep a healthy body, and so I decided never to retire completely. I reflected on the good people I had known who had retired at the age of 60, and the very short time they had lived to enjoy their retirement. In particular, a bank manager friend of mine who had worked very hard and brilliantly suddenly relinquished interest in all the things that had previously given him an active and exciting life. He surrendered completely, just reading, watching television and going for walks. He barely lasted 12 months. And another close friend who had worked very hard in the police force and attained a very high position, said on retirement that he would never do another stroke of work, not even the garden. I don't think he lived two years. And I could go on citing people who have suddenly turned off any strenuous mental activity to the complete detriment of their physical wellbeing.

In short, I believe that one must continue to stretch one's mind as hard as possible as long as possible to keep well and happy.

The other important thing is to think young, and never to say 'I am too old to do this or that'. I think it is important to accept every challenge at almost any age, unless one has physical disabilities that prevent it. To grow old gracefully, I think one needs to indulge in a certain amount of self discipline, cutting out cocktail parties, drinking and smoking modestly, taking frequent and regular exercise and eating as little as possible. I think diet has a very great deal to do with it, especially a high fibre diet. And it is important that the older you get, you should be careful not to distress yourself with imaginings, for many fears are born of fatigue and loneliness.

So beyond the wholesome discipline I have touched upon, which has been well said before, be gentle with yourself, remembering that you are a child of the universe, no less than the trees and the stars and that you have a right to be here. And whether or not it is clear to you, no doubt the universe is unfolding as it should. Therefore be at peace with God, whatever you conceive Him to be, and whatever your labours and aspirations have been in this world and in the noisy confusion of life, keep peace with your soul; for in spite of everything and age and illness with all its sham, drudgery and broken dreams, it is still a beautiful world. So strive to be happy.

Yours sincerely

*Julian Hodge.*

◇◆ ◇◆ ◇◆ ◇◆ ◇◆ ◇◆ ◇◆ ◇◆ ◇◆ ◇◆

**Lord Bullock** FBA. **Born 13 December 1914.**

Founding Master and Fellow, St Catherine's College,
Oxford; Vice Chancellor, Oxford University, 1969-73.

◇◆ ◇◆ ◇◆ ◇◆ ◇◆ ◇◆ ◇◆ ◇◆ ◇◆ ◇◆

Dear Mr Bristow

I know perfectly well what to say to people over the age
of seventy who have kept their health; have lived an
energetic and fairly successful life, and have had a good
education. I have no idea what to say to people over
seventy who have not had the good fortune to enjoy
these blessings. Of course there are many people who
have had none of these things, and who put those of us
who have to shame by the example they set by their
serenity and constant willingness to help others. But
there are also others, I suspect those whom you are
trying to reach, who fall into neither of the two
categories I have mentioned. I honestly don't know what
to say to them.

If they have never read books or tried to learn
something, it is very unlikely they would start now. If
they have not got good health and are not amongst those
who can somehow or other rise above that condition; and
if their experience in life has been one of disappointment
or failure, or just plain humdrum, what can one say?

I feel that those of us who are fortunate enough to have
enjoyed the things I have spoken of, owe a debt and
ought to be able to help those who have not.

Yours sincerely

*Alan Bullock*

— ◆ ◇ ◆ —

## Elizabeth Longford CBE.
## Born 30 August 1906.

Authoress.
Best-selling titles include:
*Victoria RI* and *Wellington,
Years of the Sword.*

— ◆ ◇ ◆ —

Dear Mr Bristow

I should have written to you quite differently if I had seized my pen a few months ago. Up till last Christmas I was a hale and hearty 82-year-old. I walked fast, weeded my garden, carried heavy water cans.

True, I had been on a fat-free diet for the past three years. But I had managed to forget the difference between margarine and butter, skimmed milk and cream. Anyway, why be nostalgic about food? My diet had banished the dreaded gallstones – and still does. My problem was to realise how old I was and not to go on behaving like a skittish 50-year-old.

You may ask, why try? Because you can't reap the full benefits of old age if you go on too long aping the features of youth. And what are those benefits? More time for thought, reading, companionship, remembering, appreciating the gifts that still come one's way. The bliss of not having to bother about superficial things; not having to traipse from shop to shop, indecisive and disappointed by the failure of all those dresses to please. Instead, mail orders deserve the order of merit for services to the old. No one will love you less for wearing old favourites more. I am lucky in having seven children, 26 grand-children and one great-grand-child in whom to renew my own sense of youth. But even without one's 'own' children, there are always ways of using one's years in the service of the young. They all love stories about the past. The way things were in, say, George V's days seem to them stranger than fiction. Or write them letters. You will get some surprising answers.

Then fate suddenly struck last Christmas. One day I was decorating the Christmas tree; the next I could hardly turn over in bed or crawl down stairs. A spinal operation kept me in hospital for six weeks and now, six months since the op, I still have to walk with two sticks outdoors, one stick in the house. (When I see a two-sticker in the House of Lords I am apt to call out 'Race me!') But I hope to get rid of my second stick, soon. You remember the saying of the pigs in *Animal Farm*, 'Four legs good, two legs bad'? I have adapted it: 'Two sticks bad, one stick good'. I can enjoy pool therapy, drive my car sporting an orange label and carry some of my shopping in a bag worn round the neck like an old cab-horse's nose-bag.

If you are handicapped as well as old, cling on for dear life to your remaining independence and relics of youth. Dress better than before, never miss a hair-do, accept all invitations despite the effort. This cheers your family. Then, to cheer yourself, take up something new. For instance, thousands of people were rather good at painting when at school, and then dropped it. It's one of the best things to pick up again. And something to start, or re-start, is a diary.

Yours sincerely

Elizabeth Longford

## Sir Alec Rose.
## Born 13 July 1908.

Circumnavigated the world
in My Lively Lady, 1968.

Dear Mr Bristow

I can only say that I have found that it is in giving out of
friendship and courtesy that one finds results. The act of
giving of oneself and of one's time results in the peace of
mind and contentment that we all look for as we get
older. This applies to all walks of life – rich or poor. One
does not have to be rich to achieve this. I know of rich
people who are friendless in the real meaning of
friendship, except for a few hangers on. I also know and
count among my good friends people of modest means
just living on their pension and within their income who
are surrounded by friends just because they do not
complain and are always ready to lend a helping hand to
a neighbour. People who are always complaining are the
friendless ones.

So, I say always keep as active as possible, wear a smile
and the hand of friendship and the rewards will be great
in the response one receives. The giver is always more
blessed than the receiver.

Yours sincerely

Alec Rose

◇◆ ◇◆ ◇◆ ◇◆ ◇◆ ◇◆ ◇◆ ◇◆ ◇◆ ◇◆

# Professor Herbert C Brown PhD.
## Born 22 May 1912.

Wetherill Research Professor Emeritus,
Purdue University.
National Medal of Science, US Government, 1969;
Nobel Prize in Chemistry, 1979.

◇◆ ◇◆ ◇◆ ◇◆ ◇◆ ◇◆ ◇◆ ◇◆ ◇◆ ◇◆

Dear Mr Bristow

Following my retirement at age 66 (1978), instead of retiring to a life of ease and vegetation, I accepted the invitation of Purdue University to continue my research activities, even though I would no longer receive a salary.

During my 'retirement', I was awarded the Nobel Prize for Chemistry (1979), followed by many other prestigious awards. In my youth it was thought that scientists did their best work before age 35. It was then downhill. Accordingly, my wife had agreed to give me every possible opportunity to do such creative work by age 35 by relieving me of all routine duties. She would handle the bills as well as the housework. As I continued to do creative work past 35, I apologised. But she rejected my apology. She had enjoyed our joint efforts and had no regrets. Indeed, her responsibilities had their compensation. When we went to Stockholm to receive the Medal and the Award, she let me carry back the Medal, but she took charge of the $100,000 Award.

Ability is Ageless.

Sincerely

*Herbert C. Brown*

◆ ◇ ◆

## Cardinal Basil Hume CMG, FRCP.
## Born 2 March 1923.

Roman Catholic Archbishop
of Westminster.

◆ ◇ ◆

*Dear Mr Bristow*

*This life is a period of training, a time of preparation, during which we learn the art of loving God and our neighbour, the heart of the Gospel message, sometimes succeeding, sometimes failing.*

*Death is the way which leads us to the vision of God, the moment when we shall see Him as He really is, and find our total fulfilment in love's final choice.*

*The ultimate union with that which is most lovable, union with God, is the moment of ecstasy, the unending 'now' of complete happiness. That vision will draw from us the response of surprise, wonder and joy which will be forever our prayer of praise. We are made for that.*

*Yours sincerely*

◇ ◇◆ ◇◆ ◇◆ ◇◆ ◇ ◇◆ ◇◆ ◇◆ ◇◆ ◇

## Lord Murton of Lindisfarne PC, OBE, TD.
## Born 8 May 1914.

Member of Parliament, 1964-79.
Deputy Speaker, House of Lords.

◆ ◇◆ ◇◆ ◇◆ ◇◆ ◇◆ ◇◆ ◇◆ ◇◆ ◇

Dear Mr Bristow

Those whose beliefs are strongly rooted in Christian doctrine are best able to cope with the onset of old age. There are many words of comfort for those willing to read them.

Those who remain bitter and angry can only suffer a gradual deterioration in their mental and physical condition.

The fortunate ones are those who have, all their working life, cultivated a hobby which can be pursued in advancing years. There is danger for those who have no interest outside their work.

The greatest temptations in modern living are the cosy armchair and the television set. It is all too easy to sink into the one and stare in a state of semi-hypnosis at the other.

Physical exercise is important. Mine is compulsory because we have a dog and feel all the better for it – the dog and the walk.

The elderly should not shut themselves indoors if they are mobile enough to get up and about. Clubs are a source of human contact and, better still, so is some form of voluntary work.

Yours sincerely

Murton of Lindisfarne

───  ◆ ◇ ◆  ───

## Terence Cuneo OBE.
## Born 1 November 1907.

Portrait and figure painter.
Well known works include studies of
the Battle of El Alamein, King George VI,
the Coronation of Queen Elizabeth II,
portraits of members of the Royal Family
and a popular series of railway posters.

───  ◆ ◇ ◆  ───

Dear Mr Bristow

Growing old is *not* amusing and I, like nearly all of us, detest
the thought of it. In fact, in my estimation science should have
got to work and thought of some way of doing away with the
wretched malady years ago. However, we're stuck with it and
sooner or later the dreaded affliction will get its claws into
each and every one of us. But is it inevitable that we must lie
back in gloomy resignation and let so-called old age take us
over? *I most certainly do not think so.*

Firstly we must become occupied, involved in some outside
interest. What that interest is is relatively unimportant. But
let's do *something* and keep going at it. The great thing, I'm
convinced, is to become aware that the something you are
doing is important to somebody else other than yourself.
That's the thing and I believe in this implicitly. Yes I know
some of you will be saying to all this, 'But I'm old, nobody
really gives a damn whether I'm alive or dead', or 'I haven't the
energy' or 'There's nothing I can do that would interest
anyone' or, 'I've tried all sorts of things and nothing seems to
help - it's hopeless' or 'Nobody takes me seriously, I'm just a
has been'. And so on. Believe me I understand only too well
how many of you feel. Damn it, I should do, I'm in my 81st
year. But we've all got to fight this, you know – and we can.

I'm an artist by profession. God has given me a truly wonderful
life which is as exciting today as it was fifty years ago. But it

hasn't been altogether easy to maintain this excitement. As one gets older the tendency is to ease off, take on less work or do a little more relaxing in deckchairs in the sunshine. This tendency I have fought against vigorously and today as an eighty-year-old I am almost as active as I was at 30 *and* as much involved. I'm aware, of course, of one great advantage my profession gives me: I need never retire; whilst so very many of us have to. In other words it's easy for me to talk. But then, I've known so many people who have longed for retirement, to enable them to take up some work or hobby they have been waiting for years to be in a position to do. These are the people who are fortifying themselves against the miseries of old age. If you should not be one of these lucky ones *do please* give a thought to what I have, rather clumsily, tried to say and God bless you.

Yours sincerely

*Terence Cuneo.*

—— ♦ ◇ ♦ ——

## Michael Foot PC, MP.
## Born 23 July 1913.

Member of Parliament,
1945-55, since 1960.
Secretary of State for Employment,
1974-76; Lord President of the Council
and Leader of the House of Commons,
1976-79; Leader of the Labour Party,
1980-83.

—— ♦ ◇ ♦ ——

Dear Mr Bristow

My own pattern of activity helps me to keep from feeling
old or too old – walking my dog four or five miles each
morning on Hampstead Heath, before most people are
out and about. And, in addition to going back and forth
to my constituency – and that takes up a great deal of my
time – I try to fill in the gaps by reading. I would like
more time for that activity.

But I fear this may not be very helpful guidance. I do
believe one has to *think* positively in all these matters –
but that goes for the whole of life, and not just for the
later years.

Yours sincerely

*Michael Foot*

◆ ◇◆ ◇◆ ◇◆ ◇◆ ◇◆ ◇◆ ◇◆ ◇◆ ◇◆

**Odette Hallowes** GC, MBE, Legion d'Honneur.
**Born 28 April 1912.**

Formerly Odette Churchill.
Served in Special Forces, 1939-45 War.
Worked in France as British Agent
until captured by Gestapo;
sentenced to death 1943,
endured imprisonment and torture
at Ravensbruck Concentration Camp
until liberation in 1945.

◆ ◇◆ ◇◆ ◇◆ ◇◆ ◇◆ ◇◆ ◇◆ ◇◆ ◇◆

Dear Mr Bristow

I should like to be able to help with something positive,
but I believe everybody reacts differently to all sorts of
problems, including old age.

It is fortunate of course, if one has a family and friends,
but even if they have, the disabilities of old age can make
you feel you want to retire into a quiet corner, as it is
possible to feel that one has become a burden to one and
all.

I think this is the trouble of unselfish and sensitive old
people. I am afraid I have no very useful advice, but I do
think that most of all it is of the greatest importance to
keep contact with people.

In a sense, even money cannot always relieve loneliness
and one should not hesitate to seek friendship.

Yours sincerely

*Odette Hallowes*

◆ ◇ ◆

**Lord Scarman PC, OBE.**
**Born 29 July 1911.**

Judge.
Lord of Appeal
in Ordinary, 1977-86.

◆ ◇ ◆

*Dear Mr Bristow*

*Walk, think, act, read and talk as long and as often as you can. If you have a cause, dedicate yourself to it; if you garden, ditto; and if you have a family, ditto.*

*If you have a cause, garden and a family you should find old age an exhilaration.*

*That is my prescription.*

*Your sincerely*

Leslie Scarman

## Mary Lutyens FRSL. Born 31 July 1908.
### Daughter of Sir Edmund Lutyens.
### Writer.

Dear Mr Bristow

I wish I could think of some infallible way to help the old from boredom, despair, etc. I imagine boredom is the main problem. If their minds are occupied they are more likely to forget themselves. The bright, cheerful ones are usually the outgoing type who have always been interested in other people and in helping them.

The least bored old people I know are those who still have the imagination to go on writing or practising some other form of art. Others are those who have kept on dancing in some form. Those who have kept their minds and interests alive are the card players. Quite dim people can enjoy whist, if not bridge. And then there are lots of other, simpler card games. For someone who lives alone there are numerous forms of patience or jigsaw puzzles, or crosswords. Then there are books – or tapes or records for those who like being read to. And what about making soft toys or patchwork quilts for those who enjoy sewing?

If the old have become vegetables, or almost vegetables, one cannot think of any way to help them. But for those who still function mentally I imagine the great thing is to keep busy. I suppose a great deal depends on their state of health, but they won't notice their infirmities so much if their minds are occupied.

I am afraid there is little help for you in what I have written. I look forward to reading your book. It may help me. I shall be 81 in July and am very lucky in still loving my writing and in having a wonderful husband of 84 who is as busy as I am.

Yours sincerely

Mary Lutyens

**Lord Callaghan** KG, PC.
**Born 27 March 1912.**

Member of Parliament, 1945-87.
Chancellor of the Exchequer, 1964-67;
Home Secretary, 1967-70;
Secretary of State for Foreign and
Commonwealth Affairs, 1974-76;
Prime Minister and First Lord
of the Treasury, 1976-79.

Dear Mr Bristow

The most important foundation for an enjoyable old age is good health. Blessed with that, all doors remain open and although physical disability increasingly restricts the activities of most, I have no doubt that positive thinking, with a determination to make the best of things, is the most successful way to keep old age in its place.

Also, never stop developing new interests and have as wide a spread as you can. As the next generation takes over the world must change, so keep your curiosity alive with regard to what is happening. Do not give up learning about new things and do not remain stuck in the mud with your long-formed ideas and prejudices. Listen to what the young have to say and give their views a fair hearing.

Finally, always keep your eyes open for ways to help good causes and other people. You may not be able to do much but it is the will that counts.

Yours sincerely

James Callaghan

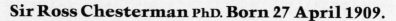

# Sir Ross Chesterman PhD. Born 27 April 1909.

Warden of Goldsmiths' College, 1953-74.

Dear Mr Bristow

There are very few human beings who are naturally solitary and who enjoy living alone. Many older people are greatly helped by the companionship of pets. But this is rarely an effective substitute for human friendship. Yet we are, as we age, losing old friends – by distance, or death – so now is the time to take every possible step to build up new relationships – perhaps by joining church, clubs, societies, bingo, etc. Coach outings and dances for the elderly can lead to friendships especially if followed up by writing (exchange addresses) – try also writing to the local paper. Pen-friends are better than no friends, and may lead to the real thing. Don't depend on television, which especially for the bored or despairing will usually make things worse; radio is better.

Providing you are not too infirm, voluntary social work, eg with church, hospitals or clubs, offers not just companionship but a realisation that one *can* be of use in the world. To encounter situations even more testing and unpleasant than our own may help to put these in perspective.

In growing old, I myself made many bad avoidable mistakes, so I speak from experience. My first wife and I retired from a satisfying and busy academic life in London to what appeared to be a dream cottage in beautiful country; yet we now found ourselves cut off from all our friends and interests. My wife was sensible enough to join the county orchestra and various literary classes. I depended on my major hobby, painting (a solitary occupation) and which because of my increasing depression got steadily worse. Occasional continental holidays gave some respite, but only temporarily.

The death of my wife made life really dreadful and I suffered four bleak years of despair. Understandably I have real sympathy for those in a similar situation. But I am lucky, for a second happy marriage and a return to the north of England have given me a new lease of life which I now greatly enjoy. Such simple pleasures as gardening, bird-watching and exploring the local countryside together give real contentment.

Surprisingly, I find now that I welcome the numerous visitors who come to see us. I have a shrewd idea that in general the despairing and unhappy are not specially welcome, either as visitors or hosts. Certainly the friendly north country people help. I find myself responding to their cheerful smiles – a conditioned reflex? Perhaps, but an effective way of warming a cold heart.

Yours sincerely

*Ross Chesleman*

## Rear Admiral Sir Matthew Slattery
### KBE, CB, FRAeS.
## Born 12 May 1902.

Director Air Material, Admiralty, 1939-41;
Director-General,
Naval Aircraft Development and Production, 1941;
Managing Director, Short Bros and Harland, 1948-52;
Chairman, Bristol Aircraft, 1957-60;
Chairman, BOAC, 1960-63.

Dear Mr Bristow

I think it is a great mistake when people retire too young; that is if retiring implies putting one's feet up and doing virtually nothing. It is essential to keep going both mentally and physically, only gradually reducing the level of one's activity as age progresses. Exercise is essential. Swimming is very good and so is walking if one is able. Gardening is also good but should not be overdone.

I retired at 80 but still do up to three or three and a half hours in the garden when the weather is possible. As one gets older one does not seem to need so much food – so eat lightly avoiding too much fat or fried foods. I do not smoke because I no longer like it but I drink alcohol in modest quantity. Keep warm at all times but keep in the fresh air as much as possible.

Yours sincerely

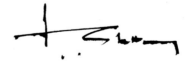

— ♦ ◇ ♦ —
# Sir Hardy Amies KCVO, RDI, FRSA.
## Born 17 July 1909.

Director, Hardy Amies Ltd.
Dressmaker by
Appointment to HM The Queen.

— ♦ ◇ ♦ —

Dear Mr Bristow

1.   I believe in homeopathic medicine in the sense that its practitioners try to find the cause of an illness or discomfort before prescribing a remedy. There is no need to be a fanatic. Antibiotics are useful in emergencies, but care should be taken to dispel the effects of such poisons by homeopathic means.

2.   Exercise is essential and if this is taken through sport such as tennis or golf it can be very interesting.

3.   A life enhancing hobby such as gardening or needlepoint (me) is more than useful.

4.   You have time to listen to records and the radio and to see television. Careful selection is essential.

5.   Experience should bring wisdom: this should mean control of the tongue, making reproaches or complaining should only be used if there is a real chance of correcting or improving an irritating situation. It is the duty of the old to bring peace to the young.

6.   A delicate subject. An interest in sex should not be suppressed by the old. Nature is very generous and has included gerontophiles in her caste of characters.

Yours sincerely

*Hardy Amies*

*Dear Mr Bristow*

*I'm afraid I haven't at all come to terms
with getting old myself — in fact I refuse
to accept it.*

*So I can't be any help to you, but I will
buy the book.*

*Good wishes from*

*Wendy Toye*

♦ ◇ ♦

## Deborah Kerr.
## Born 30 September 1921.

Stage and screen actress.
Film credits include:
*Black Narcissus,*
*From Here to Eternity*
and *The King and I.*

♦ ◇ ♦

Dear Philip Bristow

What an interesting idea for a book which, I'm sure, will help many older people come to terms with their advancing years.

We all, of course, grow old and as there is absolutely nothing we can do to prevent this – we can only accept it and make the most of what is left of our lives. It is all too easy to sink into lethargy and despair, especially if we find ourselves coping with ill health we never had before, or aching bones, etc! It is easy to give up and do *nothing* but, of course, this is the wrong attitude entirely. An active mind and body is the key to youthfulness, no matter how old we have the good fortune to grow to be. We should be grateful for our long lives, for so many people are deprived of this chance, and we should look upon every extra year we are granted as a bonus!

So...keep up some kind of a social life – see people – make new friends – be interested in the lives of others! Keep your mind active – read – take up a hobby if you don't have one already! And, keep moving – exercising – if you can. Even a short walk can be beneficial!

Having read what I have written I realize that I do not always practice what I preach! But the important thing is to TRY.

Yours most sincerely

*Deborah Kerr*

◇◆ ◇◆ ◇◆ ◇◆ ◇◆ ◇◆ ◇◆ ◇◆

## **Sir Kenneth Cork GBE, FCA, DLitt.**
## **Born 21 August 1913.**

Vice-Chairman, Ladbroke Group.
Lord Mayor of London, 1978-79;
Governor,
Royal Shakespeare Theatre.

◇◆ ◇◆ ◇◆ ◇◆ ◇◆ ◇◆ ◇◆ ◇◆

Dear Mr Bristow

I am not sure I am qualified to advise and guide other people as to how to deal with growing old!

I think the main thing is to live each day as it happens, and see that you have, hopefully, some sort of business interest which you enjoy and keep playing at, – and I mean playing – and do other things, such as Charity or the Arts, where you can give the benefit of your experience to other people.

I think if I were to stay at home all day and do nothing but plod around the garden, I would be dead within three months! I may well be dead in three months, but at least I will have enjoyed those three months!

Kindest regards,

Yours

**Lord Forte** FRSA.
**Born 26 November 1908.**

Chairman,
Trust House Forte plc.

*Dear Mr Bristow*

*Perhaps I can best sum up my attitude to life and health by quoting from my autobiography:*

*'You should have good feelings about things and people. If you do, you have a chance of being healthier. If you do not, debilitating tension arises'.*

*Sincerely,*

## Lord Beloff DLitt, FBA.
## Born 2 July 1913.

Professor Emeritus and Fellow Emeritus,
All Souls College, Oxford University.

Dear Mr Bristow

I have considered your interesting letter and much as I would like to help, I am not sure that I have anything interesting to say. I would have thought that the main reasons for unhappiness in old age are often outside the individual's control. The essentials for having a positive outlook on life must surely be continuing good health and an income enough to enable a reasonably comfortable life to be had, with adequate food, heating and something over for whatever occupations or hobbies give pleasure. Many no doubt would feel that religious faith is also helpful and perhaps essential.

From your letter I would think that what may concern you is not old age as such but retirement. It does seem to me that some people used to a full life in employment find it hard to fill their time when nothing calls them to go out to a job. I would have thought that there are plenty of opportunities in local affairs and in voluntary organisations for keeping oneself busy.

Many people, I am sure, myself included, who have had a rather busy life in employment must have saved up or postponed a lot of things they would like to have done but have not had time for.

Very sincerely yours

## Mother Teresa MC, Hon OM, Hon OBE.
## Born Skopje, Yugoslavia,
## 27 August 1910.

Roman Catholic nun.
Founder the Missionaries
of Charity (Sisters), 1950.

Dear Mr Bristow

Growing old is a gift from God – we can count the years, the hours, the minutes of how long we have had to love Jesus. And loving Jesus is not just the luxury of a few but a simple duty for each of us, young or old. And how can we love Jesus? By loving each other with a pure heart. And the fruit of love is service. There are so many ways in which we can serve one another. It does not matter what we do or how much we do, but how much love we put into the doing. Jesus Himself tells us, 'Whatever you do to the least of my brethren you do unto me'. Just a simple smile, companionship to one another, serving the poor in small and simple ways, by using the talents and experience which growing old gives each of us.

My prayer for you will be that you may continue to keep the joy of loving Jesus ever burning in your heart and share that love with all you meet.

Please remember me, my sisters and the poor we serve in your prayers.

*God bless you*
*lee Teresa me*

## Moura Lympany CBE, FRAM.
### Born 18 August 1916.
International concert pianist.

Dear Mr Bristow

First, I don't think of myself as OLD. I keep active, never stop working, have a lot of hobbies and don't have the time to think that I am old, tired, unhappy, helpless — none of which I am anyway.

The great thing is to be so busy that you have no time to think about whether you are old, unhappy, etc... .

Anyway, I have so many projects that keep me busy and happy.

Sincerely,

*Moura Lympany*

## George P Shultz.
## Born New York,
## 13 December 1920.

United States Secretary
of State, 1982-89.

Dear Mr Bristow

A few years ago when I was in Germany, I had a talk with
my good friend the late Arthur Burns. He had just been
appointed US Ambassador to Germany. He told me how
excited he was to be learning a new language and to be
exploring the culture of a new country. He was 78 years
old and acted like a youngster with a new toy.

I have taken a lesson from Arthur Burns as I grow older
myself. The lesson is that if you're willing to learn, there
are new things all around you. The act of learning keeps
you alive and vital.

Sincerely yours

*George P Shultz*

85

# Air Vice Marshal A. A. Adams CB, DFC.
# Born 14 November 1908.

Chief of Staff, Far East Air Force, 1957-59;
Director, Mental Health Trust and Foundation,
1970-77.

Dear Philip Bristow

Until we moved to Eastbourne last year to enjoy less
arduous living in a flat, I had not realised that old age
was upon me. My wife and I had been busy with a small
orchard and garden in the Cotswolds and had not noticed
the flight of time since I retired from business at the age
of seventy. Then I was also a District Councillor. So, I
suppose the first advice I would give would be to
deliberately seek interests that keep one fully occupied.

Now in my 80th year, being no longer quite so mobile, I
am interested in collecting coins and am a director of a
property company. Again it must be a matter of doing
something rather than just sitting around. Travel, of
which I have done a lot in my time, might suit those who
don't like work. They would find plenty to occupy
themselves, the planning, the hustle, the enjoyment of
change and later the showing of snapshots.

Then I think it is a good thing to have a philosophy of
life, to feel happy in a sound knowledge of what it is all
about. Not necessarily religion, but that itself can help.

Yours sincerely

*Alec Adams*

**Lord Delfont.
Born Tokmak, Russia,
5 September 1909.**

Theatrical impressario.
Life President,
Entertainment Artistes'
Benevolent Fund.

———— ◆ ◇ ◆ ————

*Dear Mr Bristow*

*Much as I would like to help with your
book I do not consider that I am old —
not yet! Just approaching middle age.*

*Seriously, I have always worked at
something I enjoy which may be the
answer and the only advice I can give is
to keep active.*

*Yours sincerely*

87

Dear Mr Bristow

In relation to the problem of aging, when you seek advice for guidance in relation to this generally unhappy state a viewpoint may only be expressed on the basis of the health of an aging person.

Should one be in reasonably good health when they reach four score years, they can remain fairly active. If health is very poor at four score years, then they have got to be exceedingly careful, even in walking, quite aside from food intake and activities of which they may be capable.

Perhaps I should have started with commenting on those who reach the age of 65, although I might add that I am very disappointed that too many people are forced into retirement at the age 60 and I think that it is far too young to want to retire. As a matter of fact, there are businesses that require people to retire at the age of 60 and if one is in good health at that time, they are in danger of getting into trouble because of inactivity, but they can, of course, seek another activity.

It has been my observation that inactivity in an aging person is dangerous because of despair and boredom. Most of all, mental activity and stimulation is truly mandatory, even if you are only reading books.

Sincerely

Walter Annenberg

―― ♦ ◇ ♦ ――

# Dave Brubeck. Born California, 6 December 1920.

Musician and composer.
Founder, Dave Brubeck Quartet;
composer of *Take Five*.

―― ♦ ◇ ♦ ――

Dear Mr Bristow

Advice to the elderly is difficult to give, because each has lived a full life and unlike a child, character and personality are fully formed. However, I believe it is possible to modify one's personality by a *conscious* effort to think through one's philosophy and thereby avoid slipping into an unconscious, unthinking, negative attitude.

We are given the precious spark of life, and therefore are part of all humanity. To respond to life with affirmation, no matter how restricted our lives may have become physically, is to contribute to the solution of the human dilemma on the positive side rather than adding weight to the negative. Affirmation to me, means a commitment to other people, and life-long study and appreciation of the arts, and continued enjoyment in hobbies and activities as long as our strength and health permits. It is now a scientific fact that people, who consistently do for others, suffer far less from depression and minor ailments. The very act of giving of oneself stimulates a measurable physical response within the body. There are many people in this world, especially children, who need attention, caring and loving, and who would respond with joy to the companionship of an elderly person or a surrogate grandparent or parent. There are such programs in America, matching up young people with the elderly in homes, and it has proven to be very effective.

In summation, my advice would be: 'Don't give up being your own person...a human being...just because you are old in years. Remain youthful in spirit, by loving, giving and caring'.

Yours sincerely

*Dave Brubeck*

Dear Mr Bristow

There is no such thing as growing old. Old is ten years
more than your present age, and young is ten years less.

The actual point of retirement for many people is a
watershed. A time of mixed emotions of achievement,
relief and anticipation.

My suggestion to make the most of the remaining years
is to take on extraneous jobs, either mental or physical,
which carry broad interests without too much detailed
responsibility. Experience is of tremendous value if
passed on to a younger generation as tactful
consultation rather than 'I am telling you' instructions.

Above all, for continuation of a happy married life,
always stay out for lunch.

Yours sincerely

## Sir Bernard Braine PC, DL, MP.
## Born 24 June 1914.

Member of Parliament since 1950;
"Father of the House".

Dear Mr Bristow

There is a proverb which runs 'for the ignorant old age is
as winter, for the wise it is a harvest'. Inevitably we reap
what we have sown. As we grow older therefore the
secret is never to allow ourselves to lose enthusiasm but
to keep the mind fully stretched and to go on learning
something new every day. Circumstances often cut us
off from contemporaries, our friends and loved ones, but
we need never feel completely isolated. With a good book
one is never alone; with even a small garden one has an
absorbing interest.

The enemy, of course, is loneliness and the feeling that
one is no longer needed. It need not be so. We can, if we
choose, reach out to other people. After all there are
plenty of good causes and voluntary organisations in
our midst crying out for helping hands. The old, better
than the young, should know that giving is always more
rewarding than receiving.

Yours sincerely

Bernard Braine

## Professor Cyrus H Gordon. Born 29 June 1908.

Professor of Hebrew;
Director, Center for Elba Research,
New York University.

Dear Mr Bristow

I venture the following advice to the aging who don't want to be old.

Avoid exposure to senility, illness and gloom. Try to cultivate an atmosphere including the young and the middle aged as well as your peers. The young are often quicker and brighter than we, but we are more experienced and wiser than they. We can profit from each other. Be interested in the welfare and development of the young, but don't stop enjoying and nurturing your own gifts.

If you are among the lucky to have a long-term and enduring interest, keep fostering it. While you may be slowing down in acquiring new skills, you will probably be able to function more deeply and creatively in the area of your expertise.

Don't retire before you have to, and when you do retire, keep active in your calling. As long as you are learning and thinking and doing what is within your power, you may be growing older (like everyone else, from birth) but you are not old.

Attend to serious health problems promptly, but don't dwell on health. Think healthy and think young.

No intelligent senior citizen should fear death. Instead, wish that your mind does not go before your body. Death is the only release from the problems and woes of life. If you are fortunate, you will die in your sleep after an active day. Meanwhile think of life and make every day count.

The greatest of gifts is life and those blessed with years should enjoy every day 'under the sun'.

It is an error to dream of a distant retirement paradise. A person who has always used his mind may not be happy living out his 'golden years' in a condominium where retired couples are playing cards and golf. In general one should remain in one's own element. Avoid unnecessary moves, and if you must move, make sure the new home is in a place where you will have what you need. I know a frustrated scholar who retired to a beautiful home on the posh island of Hilton Head, where, however, there is no library with the books and journals he needs, nor any community of scholars with whom he can discuss his interests. His is a paradise for retired tycoons but not for him.

Keep your independence as long as you are competent to manage your own affairs. Don't relinquish the control of assets that you may need to avoid dependence on others.

The world is changing more rapidly than ever in this era of exploding knowledge and technology. In times gone by, there were 'Renaissance men' of amazing breadth and versatility. Today we have instead 'Renaissance ignoramuses' who are equally ignorant in many fields. But beware of telling young people that the quality of humanity is declining. While we remain cognizant of the virtues of our generation, don't be oblivious of the gigantic strides made in recent times. Hippocrates and Osler were better all-around physicians than those our medical schools turn out today, but if you need a heart transplant or brain surgery, our superb (albeit narrow) specialists today can save your life, which the medical giants of the past could not.

Build on the past but live in the present.

Sincerely yours

93

# Norman Hepple RA, RP, NEAC.
## Born 18 May 1908.

Figure subject and portrait painter.
President, Royal Society of
Portrait Painters, 1979-83.

Dear Mr Bristow

The only trouble I find about growing old is my body. I get tired easily and sleep badly, but I'm certainly not bored. I have the unfailing need to paint, it has the advantage of having no final end, it's very very difficult, and I can brood over what I've done and think about what I will do next, and tomorrow.

The answer I think for the old retired person is to find something he or she can do continually which is rather difficult and of which they can start another variant when they've finished the one in hand. Things they can make, or do; necessitating the use of the hands are best, but there must be many other occupations of an absorbing nature. If only they can get interested in whatever it may be that suits them. There are all the arts and crafts, and endless classes open that can teach them the basic knowledge. The thing is to make a start, interest will grow with the doing.

Yours sincerely

*Norman Hepple*

**Charlton Heston.
Born Illinois, 4 October 1924.**

Stage and screen actor
and director.
Film credits include:
*Ben Hur* and *El Cid*.

Dear Mr Bristow

Your letter has reached me in China
where I'm directing a play.

I haven't been asked for advice to people
in advancing years but I suspect it would
be the same that I gave my children each
day when I dropped them off for school:
do your best and keep your promises.

Cordially,

## Alexandra Danilova. Born Pskoff, Russia, 20 November 1906.

Dancer, teacher and choreographer.
Member of the Diaghileff Company, 1925-29;
Prima Ballerina,
Ballet Russe de Monte Carlo, 1938-58;
Guest choreographer of international repute.

Dear Mr Bristow

To me the important thing to always remember is to work. God has been very good to me and since my work is preparing young dancers by passing on a technique and a discipline that I learned in Russia many years ago; there is no question of boredom or despair.

I was as you know a dancer and now I preach what I practiced for many years.

There is a song in the 'King and I' – 'Getting to Know You' in which there is a line that says 'if you become a teacher, by your pupils you'll be taught'. My advice is to share with young people and they will, in turn, keep you young.

Yours sincerely

Alexandra Danilova

## Sir Matt Busby CBE.
## Born 26 May 1909.

Football Player and Manager;
President, Manchester United
Football Club.

Dear Mr Bristow

The important thing in life, I feel, is that we must all try to help one another, a friendly chat, a small note, just to let someone know that they are not forgotten can make all the difference.

I know that I am very fortunate, in that I have my family and my grandchildren who help to keep my spirits high and I also enjoy a round of golf although I do not play as energetically as I did.

The one good thing about growing old, is hopefully that you have the wisdom to approach things in a more balanced way, a smile can make someone's day, and if we all tried to keep this in mind the world would be a better place.

Take care and God bless,

*Matt Busby*

## Phyllis Calvert. Born 18 February 1915.

### Actress.

Dear Philip Bristow

I have a sister who is 80 who says she is as old as she feels – which is 20. I am 75 and I feel 100. However, the older I feel, having to cope with arthritis, deafness, catarrh and eye trouble, and all the other horrors of physical deterioration, the more I'm determined to lead a carefree life.

I've just completed five month's work at Chichester in 'The Heiress'. Tight corsets, billowing petticoats and 32 stairs to the stage, not to mention six changes of costume at each performance – so I'm now delighted to be in my own garden, in spite of the heat.

It is a great temptation to get in a rut as one gets older, and very pleasant that is, but if one can arouse oneself and climb out once in a while, the rut, when at last reached again, is even more desirable. My rut is very pleasant and I'm now pottering about doing what I want to do when I want to do it.

Yours sincerely

*Phyllis Calvert*

— ♦ ◇ ♦ —
## Viscount Tonypandy.
## Born 29 January 1909.

Member of Parliament, 1945-83.
Speaker of the House of Commons,
1976-83.

— ♦ ◇ ♦ —

Dear Mr Bristow

Retirement is a traumatic experience. Even those who see it
coming and make plans for their remaining years can still be
caught out. It is unwise to believe that habits of 40 or more
years established through a working life can suddenly be
changed.

Retirement (where health permits) should be seen as a time
for changing activities rather than for giving up all
responsibilities. This is a personal view. I can only speak of my
own experience.

When I stepped aside from the Speaker's Chair I was already
committed to work for a number of charities. At that time I had
not a glimmer of realisation of the blessings that this
commitment would bring into my life.

It is six years since I ceased to be Speaker of the House of
Commons. In retrospect I realise that the decision to use my
time constructively by voluntary service was a life-saver for
me. I have been at full stretch preaching and speaking, and
trying to help my various charities.

When I am asked whether I miss the House of Commons I
reply in all sincerity, "I try not to think about it. I do not want to
live in the past, much as I enjoyed it. I try to look to the future".

My diary is full with commitments for at least a year ahead. By thinking positively about things I have promised to do, I escape from just dreaming of the wonderful experiences I have been lucky enough to enjoy.

I am a Christian believer. This changes my perspective of life. Even in the fullness of years I am not afraid of tomorrow for I know that whatever happens to me, God is with me. It must be terrible to be old and not to believe in God's purposes for us all. However old we are we have gifts to use to the glory of God. When we cease to use these gifts we start to shrink both intellectually and physically.

Old age brings its problems. It is idle to pretend that this is not so. However, we can help ourselves by trying to think well of people around us; by feeling and showing gratitude for the kindnesses we receive; and also by setting out each new day to make someone feel that God's goodness reaches out to them.

Yours sincerely

George Tonypandy.

## David Hobman CBE.
## Born 8 June 1927.

Director, Age Concern England,
1970-87.

Dear Mr Bristow

In many ways I'm probably too young, in my early sixties, to be old. However, in others I qualify. I can write as a semi-retired pensioner, and as a grandparent, to express the great sense of satisfaction this new way of life provides in having the time to spare to do the things I want, without the restrictions of a career to act as a diversion.

Of course, being a grandparent has distinct advantages over parenting. For example, it provides a warm and loving relationship which spans past, present, and future. It's without responsibilities. At six o'clock they are someone else's again. Any signs of eccentricity, which used to be so embarrassing to our children, now become prized virtues. We actually get encouraged to misbehave.

At an occupational level, there are also considerable advantages. I now pursue what is known as a 'portfolio career'. This means I do a number of jobs for different organisations. Some are voluntary; some are paid. But I do them because they seem interesting and worthwhile; not because I have to. This means I can be much more relaxed about them than about a 'real' job where the bad news has to be taken with the good. If anything goes wrong now, we can just part company and go our own ways. It's very relaxing, and it makes the future so much more full of possibilities than it used to be when it was often very predictable.

Your sincerely

David H Hobman

◆ ◇◆ ◇◆ ◇◆ ◇◆ ◇◆ ◇◆ ◇◆ ◇◆ ◇

**Sir Georg Solti** KBE.
**Born Budapest, 21 October 1912.**

Conductor and Pianist.
Music Director, Chicago Symphony Orchestra.
Principal Conductor and Artistic Director,
London Philharmonic Orchestra, 1979-83.

◆ ◇◆ ◇◆ ◇◆ ◇◆ ◇◆ ◇◆ ◇◆ ◇◆ ◇

*Dear Mr Bristow*

*Watching my family grow up and striving always towards better quality in my work are two of the most important things to me at this point in my life.*

*Yours sincerely*

Georg Solti

— ♦ ◇ ♦ —

## Marjorie Proops OBE.

"Agony Aunt". Broadcaster and Journalist.
Woman Journalist of the Year, 1969.

— ♦ ◇ ♦ —

Dear Mr Bristow

Growing old is a matter of luck. If you achieve old age it is truly an achievement and it seems to me that the most important thing for older citizens to do is count their blessings.

I, myself, am an older citizen and whenever I feel low spirited (which is not a prerogative by any means of the elderly) I launch myself into the blessings counting game.

The most important blessing to my mind is to have a mind that is still functioning. No-one can expect an ageing body to function like that of a young person's but the mind can and should continue to work and the best way to make it work is to keep it working. I am fortunate enough to have a job to go to but if I didn't, I hope I would be able to keep my mind alert by reading not just escapist novels but newspapers and current affairs magazines so that I'd know what's going on in the world.

It is also very important to keep up appearance. This is easier for women than for men. We at least have our make up and judiciously applied it can hide a multitude of years. Men can make sure they look good by never neglecting to shave and by keeping their hair, if any, cut and styled regularly.

It is also important to pay attention to the way you dress. And never ever to get into the frame of mind of 'Well, what does it matter now what I look like, now that I'm getting on a bit'. It does matter. In other words all this boils down to taking positive action about the years rather than just letting them creep up on you and defeat you.

With kind regards,

Yours sincerely

*Marjie P.*

◇◆ ◇◆ ◇◆ ◇◆ ◇◆ ◇◆ ◇◆ ◇◆

# Randle Manwaring MA, FSS, FPMI.
## Born 3 May 1912.

Poet; author; retired company director.

◇◆ ◇◆ ◇◆ ◇◆ ◇◆ ◇◆ ◇◆ ◇◆

Dear Mr Bristow

*You are old Father William, the young man said*
*And your hair has become very white;*
*And yet you incessantly stand on your head*
*– Do you think, at your age, it is right?*
(Lewis Carroll)

Inevitably, age slows us down but, generally, we have energy for the things we really want to do. We lack the strength to perform the feats we once took in our stride, so we adjust mentally to the ability of ageing limbs. But if you think you can, usually you can and, as Rudyard Kipling put it: 'When you find you can do something, try something you can't'. Becoming old before our time is in the mind - initially and dominantly. I knew a man who was given a good pension at 52 but all he did in retirement was to take his wife for a hair-do once a week. Hitherto a very healthy man, he died within two years, of broncho-pneumonia, 'the old man's disease'.

When there are no new goals in sight, or old ones have been removed, warning signals should be heeded. Inevitably, we give up things as time goes by, but it should be a gradual process and when we want to give up everything we should pause in our tracks and say: 'Now I must do something different'. It may be bird-watching or football following, pottery or photography, the crossword or cooking but I must keep my interest in something or in several things, particularly in people because that is the most rewarding interest. The old can easily become very boring if they only talk about the past, with 'I remember' as the preface to every sentence.

For this reason, it is good to become involved with other people, whether at the bowls club, the day centre or the local hospital - there are always voluntary jobs to be done and no shortage of roles to be filled where people meet each other. To be active rather than passive is the secret of successful old age. To have more than one activity ensures that when one activity fails or we fail to meet its physical requirements, there are others remaining. Gardening may go well with chess, golf with stamp collecting, the hospital library with painting. In other words, as strength declines (it does) we cannot expect to be physically on the go all the time – and there are always household duties to be performed.

The mind dictates a programme to the body and if the mind is not fully programmed, the body may give up. Standing on your head may not be possible beyond, say 55(!) but the young man ought to get his share of surprises.

Yours sincerely

◇◆ ◇◆ ◇◆ ◇◆ ◇◆ ◇◆ ◇◆

**Reginald Bevins** PC.
**Born 20 August 1908.**

Member of Parliament, 1950-64;
Postmaster General 1959-64.

◇◆ ◇◆ ◇◆ ◇◆ ◇◆ ◇◆ ◇◆

*Dear Mr Bristow*

*My advice to older people. Keep as active as possible, physically and mentally. Take an interest in current affairs. Have a hobby, even if it's only picking the losers in the day's racing. Go walking for an hour — thereby sweetening relations between yourself and the wife in the kitchen; do a bit of shopping, dig a few weeds out of the garden – most helpful of all, read.*

*Yours sincerely*

*J.R. Bevins*

## Catherine Cookson OBE.
## Born 20 June 1906.

International bestselling
authoress.

Dear Mr Bristow

Use Your Napper

'Use your napper!' That's what Our Kate used to say to me... 'Use your napper!'.

But what advice can one give to another with regard to living out the period of what is termed one's 'old age'? As individuals, we approach it from differing backgrounds, and these seem to set the pattern of our activities and thinking.

In youth, we don't even think about getting old; it is in the fifties that it usually raises its inevitable head; so, what do most of us do but dread it?

Speaking as an individual, my first dread of it was that I might be facing it without my husband; and at 83 that dread still lies heavily upon me. Yet, I decided, some years ago, that, having only one life made up of days, I was wasting what might be my last one in worrying about something over which I had no control.

At that time, my body was giving me trouble, and I knew it always would, but my mind was clear and active.

ACTIVE. There is the crucial word with regard to old age, and I think, being so is the solution. Perhaps not the whole, but in good part, because stagnation of the mind can create boredom, and this becomes the breeding ground of depression, when loss of the will to live can take over.

Of course, when one is feeling utterly bleak and life ahead shows not a vestige of light, it doesn't seem quite the time to be told: 'Use your napper!' But, you know, and now I am speaking from experience, it is the time I could have actually hit the woman who said to me, 'Come on! We'll make a pair of gloves today.'

It took me a fortnight to make those gloves, hating every stitch of it; but it was a beginning.

'Now knit a jumper', she said.

'What!'...I couldn't knit. I could never follow a pattern...for the simple reason I had never tried.

At that stage, I recall vividly Kate's saying coming into my mind, and of my telling her, and forcefully, what to do with her napper.

KNIT A JUMPER!!! ME?

There was a faint light at the end of that black tunnel by the time I had finished that jumper. And my mind was working...I joined a writers' group.

So what am I saying? Just that you take up some pastime, even a useless one as long as it keeps your mind active. Remember, at this age you haven't *got* to prove yourself.

For myself, if I didn't have my work to concentrate on I'd go round the bend. You see, I'm rotten from the eyebrows downwards, and spend most of my time in bed... or in hospital, but as long as my mind is active I'll carry on; and there'll be another two books next year. That's with the help of God and the skill of my doctors and the prayers and good wishes of my friends and readers, not forgetting that woman who pulled me through the gloves and the jumper.

Yours sincerely

Catherine Cookson

## Edward Heath PC, MBE, MP. Born 9 July 1916.

Member of Parliament since 1950.
Leader of the
Conservative Party,
1965-75;
Prime Minster
and First Lord of the
Treasury, 1970-74.

Dear Mr Bristow

Thank you for your letter in which you ask for my advice to offset boredom in old age.

I believe institutions like the Open University have a wide range of courses geared to the more advanced in years.

As there are only occasional tutorials and one summer school a year, with most of the work done at home, it seems to me that these should offer a marvellous opportunity for the elderly to study a subject of their choice.

They will have all the time in the world to complete assignments and undertake thoughtful research.

Good luck with your researches.

Yours sincerely

Edward Heath

*Dear Mr Bristow*

*To me the issue is not a question of age but more an understanding of life.*

*On one hand there is the ageing of the arteries and medical complications, which can be left to the doctors. For the rest the great danger is the 'Me, I' which tends to diminish the human warmth. Retirement must be prepared for, as it is important to keep an activity, and a happy awareness.*

*Very sincerely*

Henri Cartier-Bresson

### Sir Hugh Casson
**CH, KCVO, RA, RDI, MA, RIBA, FSIA.**
### Born 23 May 1910.
President of the Royal Academy,
1976-84.

♦ ◇ ♦

Dear Mr Bristow

It comes as a surprise to hear oneself called 'old' for the first time but nobody ever wishes, if he is sensible, to be younger. But who is sensible? I am lucky to be healthy – at 79 – and as an artist/writer I am self-employed. I am in fact guilty of so much good fortune and to have so many friends and such a busy life. To those in pain, or lonely, or forgotten, life can, I am sure, be despairing. (A simple, practical thing is, I think, to keep clean and as elegant as you can afford in your appearance and your setting ... and you may get more visitors, it sounds flippant but isn't.)

The source of my happiness to me has been, I think, *curiosity* which destroys boredom and does not weaken with age.

Everything you encounter – people, objects, behaviour, nature is extraordinary and to find the extraordinary in the ordinary never fails to be enjoyable.

Sorry my words are so banal ... but age can be banal too.

Good luck.

*Hugh Casson*

◆◇◆ ◇◆ ◇◆ ◇◆ ◆◇ ◆◇ ◆◇ ◆◇

## William Randolph Hearst Jr.
## Born New York, 22 January 1908.

Editor in Chief, The Hearst Newspapers.

◆◇◆ ◇◆ ◇◆ ◇◆ ◆◇ ◆◇ ◆◇ ◆◇

*Dear Mr Bristow*

*At an advanced age you certainly aren't working regularly anymore and you have time to learn things you were not sure about before.*

*Providing you stay healthy, old age is just a matter of slowing down physically but certainly no reason to crumble up and feel sorry for yourself.*

*There, that's all I've got to say on the subject.*

*Most sincerely,*

— ♦ ◇ ♦ —

## Dame Frances Clode DBE.
## Born 12 August 1903.

Chairman, Women's Royal Voluntary Service,
1971-74.

— ♦ ◇ ♦ —

Dear Mr Bristow

My first piece of advice is to count your blessings every day
and to thank God for them. Though I am no longer very active
in the true sense of the word I think that because I am slow it
is probably easier for me to fill my days. I can walk slowly to
church, to the library, to shops, to the hairdresser. I still
belong to societies and I am given lifts by friends and I try to
accept them gratefully; it is more difficult to receive
graciously than to give.

I don't have television blaring all day for company but I do
read a lot. I realised as I grew older that I was short of hobbies
so I embarked on scrap books, one for each member of my
family. These books contain photographs, press cuttings, etc.

My other hobby is jam, marmalade and jelly making, useful
for presents and to sell for charity.

A few DONT'S: Try not to trot out too many reminiscences or
to repeat your best stories. Don't say you've done your share
let someone else take over; it isn't always true. Don't talk
about illnesses, past and present.

Keep a sense of humour and laugh whenever you can. 'Laugh
and the world laughs with you, weep and you weep alone.'
Banish the word 'frustrated' from your vocabulary.

Finally, if your spirits are low, do something, if you are doing
something, do something different.

Yours sincerely

*Frances Clode.*

113

## Roy Henderson CBE, FRAM. Born 4 July 1899.

Baritone Singer;
Professor of Singing, RAM, London, 1940-74;
Conductor.

Dear Mr Bristow

I am sure one of the best ways to keep cheerful in old age is to have as many interests and hobbies as your state of health will allow; *depending on yourself* as much as possible. This really means preparing for old age well before you become pensionable, with a mixture of active pursuits, like gardening, fishing (fishermen are always optimists), bowls, etc and sedentary ones for the winter months and in case you are housebound.

Nowadays, television and radio, apart from books and work with the hands, add to the many things you can enjoy, but if you can house a pet — a dog, cat or budgie are the best because you can talk to them - you have a friend when your own friends are scattered or die off.

You would find friends in many institutions that cater for the elderly, even bingo, but if you haven't already thought about it, you will find new friends in most churches. After all, if you are a true Christian you have no business to be miserable.

Yours sincerely

Roy Henderson

——— ◆ ◇ ◆ ———

## Lord Jakobovits.
## Born 8 February 1921.

Chief Rabbi
of the United Hebrew Congregation
of the British Commonwealth
of Nations.

——— ◆ ◇ ◆ ———

Dear Mr Bristow

We all seek long life and hail the medical advances which have
so spectacularly increased the average span of life. Yet, all too
often the price exacted by these advances is a corresponding
aggravation of the suffering, hardship and loneliness caused by
old age.

However, not only is ageing an inevitable process ordained by
nature, but there is usually a nett gain. Most people
presumably prefer to live another 20 or 30 years with the
resultant costs and infirmities, rather than to die prematurely
without them. Winston Churchill is reported to have said on
his 80th birthday when asked: 'How do you feel being 80?',
'Considering the alternative, very well'.

When Sir Robert Mayer, the famous pioneer of children's and
youth concerts, was about to celebrate his 100th birthday, and
a distinguished friend organised a concert to be attended by the
Queen in his honour, the friend warned him months ahead,
'Robert, if you die before your birthday I will never speak to
you again' and he lived happily and quite actively for over four
years more.

Enforced retirement can often precipitate premature physical
as well as mental decay. Who does not recall that Golda Meir,
when she was summoned to be Israel's fourth Prime Minister
at the age of 71, was a sick and tired woman, who became

rejuvenated instantly by the adrenalin of the enormous new responsibilities thrust upon her.

We should therefore encourage doing everything reasonably possible to extend the working life of men and women, in whatever capacity. We would deem it morally wrong for a father to retire from a business simply to give way for an impatient son, or for older people to step out of public life just to make room for younger blood. Let the young strive by their own efforts to establish themselves, and not climb to success on the back of their elders. It might be better for both generations.

Yours sincerely

## Dame Vera Lynn DBE.
## Born 20 March 1917.

Singer.
'The Forces' Sweetheart';
Vice President, Age Concern.

— ♦ ◇ ♦ —

Dear Mr Bristow

People are often surprised to know that I am still singing, well why not? I believe that if you are fit and able to carry on the work you have been doing all your life you should do so. I certainly don't believe you should retire just because you get to a certain age. It is most important as you get older that you keep busy. Apart from continuing to think commercially, I am able to help raise money for many charities. I am sure that this is possible for most people of retiring age. Utilise your knowledge or talent in helping others, it keeps you busy and therefore, I believe, healthy.

I have many interests apart from my career: gardening, painting, sewing, embroidery, collecting books. I think it is also important to eat right, by that I mean the right kind of food. I see that both my husband and myself have a diet of fresh vegetables, salad, fruit, wholemeal bread, brown rice (no fried foods), low fat cheese, etc and of course what I think very necessary – vitamins.

It is very important to keep the mind as well as the body active and go out and meet interesting people to talk to – go to evening classes, learn something new, you are never too old to learn.

Yours sincerely

Vera Lynn

◇◆ ◇◆ ◇◆ ◇◆ ◇◆ ◇◆ ◇◆ ◇◆ ◇◆ ◇◆

# Monica Dickens MBE. Born 10 May 1915.

Authoress of numerous bestsellers.
Founder of The Samaritans in the USA.

◇◆ ◇◆ ◇◆ ◇◆ ◇◆ ◇◆ ◇◆ ◇◆ ◇◆ ◇◆

Dear Philip Bristow

I don't know that I have anything to say that might be helpful, or anything that people don't know already.

But knowing something and following it up are two different things, and it's easy to fall into depression and disinterest, lacking self-confidence or initiative.

You can't generalise, because so much depends on an individual person's own personality. If they were not out-going and interested in other people before, they're not going to become that way when they're old. If they've always loved a lot of people and given tremendous amounts of attention and care, they'll go on doing that when they're old as far as they are physically capable.

Turning yourself outward to other people is, I daresay, the best idea always, and making yourself pleasant company to be with. Forget grumbling. Keep giving and not taking.

A final word: remember that your age is probably the only thing about you that's not your fault.

Yours sincerely

### Richard Murdoch. Born 1907.

Stage, film, television and
radio actor.
Affectionately remembered for
performances in
Much-Binding-in-the-Marsh.

Dear Mr Bristow

I am fortunate in that although I have reached the age of 80 I still have plenty of work from time to time and this means that I am not bored. Apart from which maintaining a small garden is good for one's health and peace of mind. I also play golf frequently.

My advice to anyone of retirement age who is fit and active is to take gentle gardening exercise. Those without a garden of their own can help those who have one. This can even be financially rewarding to anyone who wishes for extra pocket money.

Those fortunate enough to have a car can join a scheme of 'meals on wheels' – others can help one of the charity concerns – doing part time work in shops run by Oxfam, Age Concern or the Spastics Society.

Anyone unable to venture from home for physical reasons should develop a hobby. A friend of mine in his late seventies has taken up tapestry or embroidery and has made seat covers for his dining room chairs – each with a different pattern. However this can be expensive. Those who are clever could make patchwork quilts.

There is really no excuse for boredom. Work hard at doing something –anything.

Yours sincerely

*Richard Murdoch*

## Air Marshal Sir John Hunter-Tod KBE, CB.
## Born 21 April 1917.

Served 1939-45 Fighter Command;
Director, Guided Weapons, Ministry of Aviation, 1962-65;
Head of Engineer Branch and Director General
of Engineering, RAF, 1970-73.

Dear Mr Bristow

You astound me by contemplating including myself in any list of the Famous, though Old I accept! However, your letter has stimulated me into considering the matter; herewith a few random thoughts:

a. Don't hang on; cast everything one has been involved in away except of course one's real friends; I have given up professional societies and have not thought about aeroplanes or guided missiles since I retired 15 years ago. Looking backwards to one's day of glory is unhealthy.

b. Don't inflict oneself on one's spouse, eg go one's own way for lunch; get it and have it when you feel like it – who said I married him for better or for worse, not for lunch? Take over a part of the chores, eg do all the washing up or learn to cook.

c. Be grateful for no longer having great responsibilities; ease off by being involved in charitable committees, et al.

d. Hobbies are essential even if it is only golf. One can fill in time in many satisfying ways, eg maintenance of the house or gardening – particularly if it involves building things; one should not be put off by humble pursuits or by the fact that they have never been tried; there are many excellent and inexpensive community centres of instruction. It is only necessary to organise occupations at the outset, for nature is self adjusting: as age advances one becomes slower and fewer things fill in the day.

I don't suppose any of this is helpful, but the key must be to be grateful for small mercies and relax and enjoy oneself.

Yours sincerely

John Hunter Tod

## Gerald Ford.
## Born Nebraska, 14 July 1913.

President
of the United States
of America, 1974-77.

Dear Mr Bristow

'Growing Old' can be a most enjoyable experience if one continues a reasonable work and play schedule, combining charitable oriented public service, a little income producing activity and as much as possible physical or sports participation. Sitting in a lounge chair before a TV is no way to grow old.

Best regards,

*H. R. Ford*

## Naomi Mitchison.
## Born 1 November 1897.
### Authoress.

Dear Mr Bristow

Perhaps this would be a little encouraging to people of my age.

We are always forgetting names that we know perfectly well, but they slip away almost as we are going to use them. The names of garden flowers, the name of that nice place in Italy where we once went, the title of the book I was reading yesterday, even the name of your pet great-grandchild. Don't worry, you are not going mad. It is simply that over the years far too many names have been fed into your memory box. If the people you are talking with can't understand that, they are very stupid and should instead admire you for the many more names of interesting and important things which you remember perfectly.

Yours

*Naomi Mitchison*

## Dora Bryan.
## Born 7 February 1924.

### Actress.

Dear Mr Bristow

I've never really thought of myself as old. I don't look it or feel it. I do all the same things as I did when I was younger.

I am very lucky: I have just finished an eight month tour of 'Hello Dolly'. A musical I did in London 22 years ago, playing the same part. Now I am rehearsing for a tour of Noel Coward's 'Hay Fever'. So in my case, age has nothing to do with my life.

I pray I can continue to have good health and have the courage to face any problems that may arise in the future. As for advice, everyone is different. But I do know that prayer is the same for everyone. We need to keep in touch daily with God – our only strength.

All the best.

*Dora Bryan*

Dear Mr Bristow

As one grows old, one deteriorates physically and generally more rapidly than mentally. To this extent therefore to retain one's mental powers (doing a crossword, reading a book, listening to radio, viewing television, writing — indeed anything which occupies one's mind), must be of advantage.

With kindest regards,

Yours sincerely

Monty Finniston.

# Ian Douglas Smith GCLM, ID, MP.
## Born 8 April 1919.

Prime Minister
of Rhodesia, 1964-79.

Dear Mr Bristow

In retirement one can move away from the pressure of competitive life without ceasing to make a contribution to one's community, and thus share the satisfaction of co-operating with others in order to help others. The reward of doing a good turn – no matter how small – is one of the simple but very worthwhile pleasures of life. Moreover, having the time to ponder over the complex problems confronting mankind gives one a greater understanding of the behaviour of one's fellow men. It adds to one's maturity and wisdom, those most worthwhile qualities which cannot be purchased with money or learned at educational institutions, but are earned through contact with one's fellow men, through communication and the resultant understanding, and through experience.

In this way we can use our twilight years to enrich life, both for ourselves and those around us.

I would like to compliment you on what you are doing, and wish you every success.

Yours sincerely

*I. Douglas Smith*

## General Alexander M Haig Jr.
## Born 2 December 1924.

Supreme Allied Commander, Europe, 1974-79;
United States Secretary of State, 1981-82.

Dear Philip

You may not know but I have retired six times from various public and private offices. Today, at the age of 63, I anticipate at least two more retirements.

It has been my experience that so long as one is blessed with reasonable health (and perhaps even if not), life can become increasingly self-satisfying. It is my hope to remain physically and mentally active by constantly seeking new challenges in business or in the community. As the pace slows down, the opportunity to reflect on one's experiences and to read more intensely can, I believe, be most rewarding. Above all, the experiences of life, the good and the bad, if properly applied, guarantee a cheerful and active maturity.

Best wishes,

Sincerely,

♦ ◇ ♦

## Anna Wing.
## Born 30 October 1914.

Actress.
Starred as Lou Beale
in *EastEnders*.

♦ ◇ ♦

Dear Philip Bristow

I would say that perhaps the best advice one could give is to 'stay young' as long as possible, in the best sense of the word. I never think of 'growing old' and I have been bombarded with questions like this since I arrived at 70, which I didn't even notice as a landmark.

I think the most valuable experience is to rejoice in the *now* of life. If you reach out with warmth, the return is enormous! Keep as active as possible and keep in touch with good organisations. If you are poor, let go of pride. Don't cut yourself off from young children, they recharge the batteries if you see them for short sessions.

We all of us have uncharted and untapped strengths – if one area fails, try another. Make your home as safe as possible and always have a means of contact if you are taken ill. Leave the addresses of your nearest relatives or close friends in a prominent place in your home. Without taking unnecessary risks, try to live as adventurously as possible and pray continually for the end of man's inhumanity to man.

Yours sincerely

*Anna Wing*

## Admiral Sir Charles Madden GCB.
## Born 15 June 1906.

### Commander-in-Chief,
### Home Fleet and NATO Eastern Atlantic, 1963-65.

Dear Mr Bristow

In my view the golden rules are:

1. To take on some job. If you can't get a paid one, which is probable, take on some honorary ones. Working for charities and with volunteers is harder than working where the command structure is clear – but it is well worth while and provides you with companions of similar interests.

2. Do not leave the place where you have lived while working, and where all your friends and acquaintances are, to move to a remote district or the seaside, like Bournemouth, where you know no one and where most of those living there are even older than you.

These, I am sure, are the principles. When I left the Navy at 60 I took on unpaid work which lasted me till about the age of 75. I am now 83, fit and well but do experience some lack of occupation at times and, sadly, our only child and grandsons are in Canada which is a separation.

Yours sincerely

*Charles Madden*

**Caspar Weinberger** Hon GCVO.
**Born San Francisco,
18 August 1917.**

United States
Secretary of Defense, 1981-87.

Dear Mr Bristow

Some of the suggestions I might make would be to stay interested in many things; develop new hobbies; follow all of the rules for good health; and finally, one that is most important and most gratifying, try to be as helpful as possible to others. This final point is most important because it tends to take a lot of one's time and attention, and therefore keep one's mind off personal day-to-day worries.

Sincerely

Caspar W. Weinberger

## Prunella Stack OBE.
## Born 28 July 1914.

President, The Women's League
of Health and Beauty.

Dear Philip Bristow

I am very glad to contribute to your book because having now reached my seventh decade I understand some of the problems of growing old. I have watched teachers and members of Health and Beauty Exercise (formerly the Women's League of Health and Beauty, founded in 1930 by my mother) reach their sixties, seventies, and even eighties, and have seen how a positive outlook and a knowledge of how to train the body and preserve its health has kept them young in heart and looks.

Much depends on continuing good health and it is worth watching your diet and if possible attending an exercise class geared to your needs where you will make friends as well as improve your physique.

Old age can be a time of discovery and fulfilment. There is more leisure for hobbies, more time for friends, and more opportunity to savour at a deeper level experiences which perhaps were formerly lost in the rush of active everyday life. It is also of necessity a stripping process, but this can be viewed not as a diminishment but as a return to a state of simplicity where inessentials are pared away and space is left for wisdom and spiritual growth.

The most important thing of all is to preserve meaning – in work, in relationships, and in daily life. And this depends largely, I think, on accepting what fate sends and making the most of what one has, now in the present moment: the reality which will pass all too quickly away and become the past.

Yours sincerely

Prunella Stack

**Athene Seyler** CBE, in company with Donald Sinden and Gwen Watford, celebrating her 100th birthday.

— ◆ ◇ ◆ —

**Athene Seyler** CBE.
**Born 31 May 1889.** Actress.

— ◆ ◇ ◆ —

*Dear Mr Bristow*

*I've enjoyed my first one hundred years. As one grows older, one can see the mistakes one made when younger, and one can value again all the help one has had from loving friends. And, as I've grown older, I've become more than ever convinced of the health-giving properties of laughter.*

*Yours sincerely*

*Athene Seyler.*

# Other publications from Age Concern

A wide range of titles are published under the Age Concern imprint.

### Living, Loving and Ageing
*by Wendy Greengross and Sally Greengross*  £4.95

This book challenges the assumption that, as people grow older, sexuality is a subject of increasing insignificance. It examines emotional, psychological and personal relationships in later life.

### Grandparents' Rights
*by Jill Manthorpe and Celia Atherton*  £3.95

Due to the increasing cases of divorce, remarriage and cohabitation, many grandparents face separation from their grandchildren; this book explains just what rights such grandparents have. It includes advice on how to deal with emotional problems, the legal processes, and contains details of several self-help groups who can advise worried grandparents.

### Your Rights 1989/90
*by Sally West*  £1.50

A highly acclaimed guide to the state benefits available to elderly people. Updated annually.

### Your Taxes and Savings 1989/90
*by John Burke and Sally West*  £2.70

An invaluable guide to the complexities of the tax system as it effects those over retirement age and of the investments and saving opportunities available to them. Updated annually.

### Using Your Home as Capital
*by Cecil Hinton* £2.50

A best selling book for homeowners which gives a detailed explanation of how to capitalise on the value of your home. Updated annually.

## *Forthcoming Title*

### Life in the Sun
*by Nancy Tuft* £6.95

Longer holidays and permanent moves abroad are considered by millions every year. This book covers all the implications of such moves, including the emotional, financial, legal, medical and cultural effects. (Published January 1990.)

If you would like to order any of these titles please write to:

Age Concern (DEPT. FW1)
Freepost
Bernard Sunley House
Mitcham
Surrey CR4 9AS

# About Age Concern

Age Concern England, the publisher of this book as well as a wide range of others, provides training, information and research for use by retired people and those who work with them. It is a registered charity dependent on public support for the continuation of its work.

The three other national Age Concern organisations – Scotland, Wales and Northern Ireland – together with Age Concern England, form a network of over 1,400 independent local UK groups serving the needs of elderly people, assisted by well over 250,000 volunteers. The wide range of services provided includes advice and information, day care, visiting services, voluntary transport schemes, clubs and specialist facilities for physically and mentally frail elderly people.

**Age Concern England**
Bernard Sunley House
60 Pitcairn Road
Mitcham
Surrey CR4 3LL
Tel: 01-640 5431

**Age Concern Scotland**
54a Fountainbridge
Edinburgh EH3 9PT
Tel: 031-228 5656

**Age Concern Wales**
4th Floor
1 Cathedral Road
Cardiff CF1 9SD
Tel: 0222 371821/371566

**Age Concern Northern Ireland**
6 Lower Crescent
Belfast BT7 1NR
Tel: 0232 245729

We hope you found this book enjoyable. If so,
perhaps you would like to receive further
information about Age Concern or help us do
more for older people.

*Dear Age Concern*
*Please send me the details I've ticked below:*

*other publications*         *Age Concern special offers*

☐             ☐

*volunteer with a local group*      *regular giving*

☐             ☐

*covenant*             *legacy*

☐             ☐

*Meantime, here is a gift of*

£ _____ PO/CHEQUE or VISA/ACCESS No _____

NAME (BLOCK CAPITALS) _____

SIGNATURE _____

ADDRESS _____

_____

POSTCODE _____

Please pull out this page and send it to: **Age Concern** (DEPT.FW1)
**FREEPOST**
**Mitcham**
*no stamp needed* **Surrey CR4 9AS**